G000162452

A SHORT HISTORY OF
JERUSALEM

A SHORT HISTORY OF

JERUSALEM

ABRAHAM E. MILLGRAM

JASON ARONSON INC.
NORTHVALE, NEW JERSEY
JERUSALEM

This book was set in 12 pt. New Aster by Alabama Book Composition of Deatsville, AL and printed and bound by Book-mart Press, Inc. of North Bergen, NJ.

10 9 8 7 6 5 4 3 2 1

Library of Congress Cataloging-in-Publication Data

Millgram, Abraham Ezra
    A short history of Jerusalem / Abraham E. Millgram.
        p.   cm.
    Includes bibliographical references and index.
    ISBN 0–7657–6006–1
    1. Jerusalem—History. I. Title.
DS109.9.M56 1998
956.94′42—dc21   98–27683

Printed in the United States of America. Jason Aronson Inc. offers books and cassettes. For information and catalog write to Jason Aronson Inc., 230 Livingston Street, Northvale, NJ 07647-1726, or visit our website: http://www.aronson.com

To my late wife

Ida

An ardent lover of Jerusalem
who, in her long, pathetic illness,
found comfort in the knowledge
that she would be interred in Jerusalem

Contents

Prologue   Jerusalem, the Holy City of Judaism,
Christianity, and Islam   ix

1   Jerusalem's Early History   1

2   From the Partition of David's Empire
to the City's Fall in 586 B.C.E.   9

3   From the Babylonian Captivity to the
Hasmonean Victory   15

4   The Reign of Herod the Great   21

5   The War with Rome and the Fall of Jerusalem   29

6   The Second War with Rome   37

7   Jerusalem, a Pagan City   41

8   The Holy City of Christendom   47

9   A Holy City of Islam   55

10   The Rise of the Latin Kingdom of Jerusalem   63

11   The Fall of the Latin Kingdom of Jerusalem   77

12   Jerusalem Under the Mamelukes   85

13   Turkish Rule in Jerusalem   93

14   Jerusalem in the Nineteenth Century   105

15 The Growth of Jerusalem   121

16 The Rise of Zionism   127

17 Jerusalem Under the British Mandate   137

18 Jerusalem a Divided City   157

19 Jerusalem Reunited   173

Epilogue   Jerusalem Today and Tomorrow   193

Glossary   217

Key Dates in Jerusalem's History   223

General Bibliography in English   227

Reference Bibliography   233

Index   235

Prologue

Jerusalem, the Holy City of Judaism, Christianity, and Islam

Judaism, Christianity, and Islam are quite distinct in their fundamental concepts of God, in their credal expressions of belief, and in the ritual practice of worship. However, they are united in their attachment to Jerusalem as a central shrine city and a vital focus in their spiritual heritage. Their convictions regarding the sanctity of Jerusalem are based on their respective sacred chronicles and their historic associations with the city. For the Jews, Jerusalem is the one Holy City in the world. To be sure, three other cities, Hebron, Tiberius, and Safed assumed the status of holy cities, but they were in no way comparable to Jerusalem, the city which God had chosen "to rest His name in" (Deut. 12:5, etc.). For Christians, Jerusalem is the city wherein Jesus spent the last days of his life, and where Jesus was crucified, buried, and resurrected. For the Moslems, Jerusalem is the city to which Muhammad made his miraculous nocturnal trip on the remarkable steed, Buraq, and from which he ascended to heaven. Jerusalem thus assumed for the Moslems the status of a holy city next in

sanctity to Mecca and Medina. Though Jerusalem is a holy
city for the three faiths, the place it occupies in the hearts
of the faithful of the three religions is decisively distinct.

Jerusalem in the Jewish Tradition

The Jews, scattered throughout the world, have always
responded to Jerusalem with an extra heartbeat. Jerusalem
has been, for the Jews, not only a sacred memory but a
great hope. The City has always been associated with their
former glory, as the city of David and Solomon, the
prophets and the psalmists, Ezra and Nehemiah, Simon
the Just and Judah Maccabeus. Jerusalem is also the city of
the Holy Temple on Mount Moriah, and the city where the
Messiah will, in time, reestablish God's kingdom on earth.
The Jew prayed daily for God's return to Zion and for
the gathering of the exiles "from the four corners of the
earth."[1] Many a Jew who could not live in Jerusalem came
to the Holy City in his old age to be buried in the cemetery
on the Mount of Olives in order to be ready for the
messianic era when the dry bones will be revivified and the
kingdom of David will be reestablished. And those Jews
who managed to live in Jerusalem regarded themselves as
the fortunate of Israel. They lived in poverty, in filthy
hovels, under the corrupt government of the pashas. Yet
they daily thanked God—"Happy are we! how goodly is
our portion, how pleasant our lot; and how beautiful our
heritage!"[2]

---

1. Hertz, Dr. Joseph H., *The Authorized Daily Prayer Book*, Revised
Edition (New York: Bloch Publishing Company, 1957): 117. This
phrase appears in the prayer *Ahavat Olam*, part of the daily Morning
Service, which is recited immediately before the Confession of Faith:
Shema Yisrael.
2. *Ibid.*: 29. This is part of the Preliminary Prayers to the Morning
Service (*Shaharit*), also recited before the Confession of Faith.

Neither Christian nor Moslem could fathom the loving attachment of the Jew to Jerusalem. It was not comparable to the Christian veneration of the holy places, nor was it similar to the Moslem principle of *Dar al-Islam*. Jerusalem encompassed the Jew's religious sentiments, his national identity, his mystic yearnings, his historic memories, his hopeful aspirations, and more. Only a poet of stature can begin to delve into this mystery. The ordinary Jew, who has not been affected by the forces of assimilation, continually experiences this mystic attachment to the Holy City. He does not try to explain it, just as a mother experiences her loving attachment to her children without attempting to analyze it, let alone describe it. The powerful attachment of the Jew to Jerusalem is as baffling to the non-Jew as is the Jew's survival. It is an eternal riddle.

From Jerusalem's beginning as King David's capital and his choice of Mount Moriah as the site for the nation's central sanctuary, the city has continued uninterruptedly to hold a dual position in the Jewish tradition. It has always been conceived in Jewish religious sources, and in the folk tradition, as both the temporal and spiritual center of the nation. On the Ninth of Av, the Jews fast and mourn the fall of Jerusalem, the destruction of the Temple, and the exile of the Jewish people from their ancestral home. This complex of religion, land, city, and people has always been an indivisible composite of Jewish values. In the prayers of the Ninth of Av (and of every Sabbath), the verse "Renew our days as of old" (Lam. 5:21) serves as a refrain to one of the dirges recited by the congregation. "The days of old" are understood to mean the days when Jerusalem was both the nation's capital and its spiritual center. The faith and the fate of Israel were inextricably bound up with Jerusalem. The Holy City was not only a place where many divine events took place, but a city to which the aspirations and destiny of the Jewish people have irrevocably been tied. Jerusalem is, for the Jew, more than a sacred symbol;

Jerusalem is the memory of a noble past and the hope for a glorious future.

When the city of Jerusalem was destroyed by the Romans and the Temple was burned, the Jewish people tried desperately to restore Jerusalem and to renew its days "as of old." In a little over half a century after the disaster of the year 70, a violent revolt erupted. Jerusalem was recaptured, coins were struck, an altar was hurriedly erected on the Temple Mount, and the sacrificial rites were resumed. For a brief moment, Jerusalem's dual role as spiritual and temporal center of the Jewish people was "renewed." But Roman power prevailed; Jerusalem was not only sacked, but its very name was erased from the map. The Romans plowed over the city and built in its place a pagan city named *Aelia Capitolina*. No Jew was permitted to enter let alone reside in the new Roman city.[3]

The Romans had the power and the means to erase Jerusalem from the contemporary map, but they could not obliterate Jerusalem from the hearts of the Jewish people. The Jews remembered Jerusalem, mourned its destruction, prayed for its restoration, and were ever ready to resume its rehabilitation. One of the articles of faith formulated by Moses Maimonides stated:

> I believe with perfect faith in the coming of the Messiah, and though he tarry, I will wait daily for his coming.

The Jew was perpetually on the alert, ever ready to resume the "days of old." No wonder that so many "messiahs" arose in various parts of the diaspora, and it is not surprising that each one of these "messiahs" received not only a hearing but a following. The tragic results of these ever-recurring messianic movements is one of the saddest

---

3. See Chapter Six.

strains in the melancholy history of the two-thousand-year-old Jewish diaspora.

Jerusalem's sanctity in Judaism does not derive from the fact that the Holy Temple had been erected there by King Solomon. Had this been the case, the Jews would have been content with access to their holy place on the Temple Mount. The decisive factor in Jerusalem's sanctity in Judaism derives from God's choice of Jerusalem for its sacred role. This is repeatedly emphasized in the Book of Deuteronomy and repeated in other books of the Bible. We read in the Book of Psalms:

> For the Lord hath chosen Zion;
> He hath desired it for His habitation:
> "This is My resting place forever,
> Here will I dwell; for I have desired it" (Ps. 132:13–14).

Indeed, Jerusalem had already been chosen and sanctified when God bid Abraham to bring his son Isaac for the intended sacrifice "upon one of the mountains of which I shall tell you" (Gen. 22:2). Jewish tradition has definitively designated the site of Solomon's Temple as the mountain which God had chosen for "the binding of Isaac."

The sanctity of Jerusalem affected the life of the Jews who lived in it, and this sanctity did not depart from Jerusalem when the Temple was destroyed and the people were exiled. When the Jews lived in Jerusalem prior to the destruction of the Temple, there were special laws to safeguard the city's unique status. Among them were the laws that forbade the burial of a corpse in the city, nor was it permitted to harbor a corpse within the city overnight. No dunghill was permitted in the city, lest it defile the city's holiness. Land could not be sold there, and pilgrims were not to be charged for lodging. When the Temple stood, every Jew was enjoined to make three annual pilgrimages to Jerusalem.

Jerusalem maintained its holiness after the destruction of the Temple. This is one reason why Jews in the far-flung diaspora face Jerusalem in their prayer, and Jews who live in Jerusalem face the Temple Mount. The observant Jew does not enter upon the Temple Mount because he may not be in a state of ritual purity and may thus defile the sanctity of the sacred site. And pilgrimage to Jerusalem has remained a pious duty. Throughout the centuries, many a Jew performed the pilgrimage at the peril of his life.

When Christianity was founded, Jerusalem was its central place of holiness. But no sooner were the gentiles in the leadership than other cities became seats of ecclesiastical authority. Similarly, when Islam was founded, the faithful were instructed to turn to Jerusalem when reciting their prayers. However, when Islam spread and became strong and independent, the faithful were enjoined to turn to Mecca when reciting their prayers. Islam, like Christianity, turned away from Jerusalem and reverted to its original center, thus reducing Jerusalem's status as a holy city to a secondary position. Only for the Jews has Jerusalem always remained the foremost of sacred cities.

In the Bible, Jerusalem is a terrestrial city, the political and spiritual center of the Jewish people. The New Jerusalem of the future is also conceived as an earthbound city inhabited not only by Jews, but also by gentiles who have joined themselves to the Jewish people and to their faith: "For My house shall be called a house of prayer for all peoples" (Isa. 56:7). The Jerusalem of the future is not a place of holy sites and shrines, but a real city, as we read:

> Thus says the Lord of hosts: There shall yet old men and old women sit in the broad places of Jerusalem, every man with his staff in his hand for very age. And the streets of the city shall be full of boys and girls playing in its streets. (Zech. 8:4–5)

Even the Jewish eschatological concepts of the New Jerusalem are realistic. Jerusalem's tribulations will come to an end after a war in which God will destroy the nations who war on Jerusalem. The city will again become the capital of the kingdom, and the exiled Jews will be gathered into the city:

And the Lord shall roar from Zion,
And utter His voice from Jerusalem,
And the heavens and the earth shall shake;
But the Lord will be a refuge unto His people,
And a stronghold to the children of Israel.
So shall ye know that I am the Lord your God,
Dwelling in Zion My holy Mountain;
Then shall Jerusalem be holy,
And there shall no strangers pass through
her any more. . . .
But Judah shall be inhabited forever,
And Jerusalem from generation to generation
     (Joel 4:16,17,20).

In the prophetic utterances and in the psalms, Jerusalem is frequently spoken of as "Mother Zion" and the Jewish people are referred to as "Zion's children." These poetic expressions reflect the tender relationship between the Jewish people and their Holy City. Similar imagery is to be found in rabbinic literature, such as in the benediction recited after the prophetic reading in the synagogue:

Have mercy upon Zion, for it is the home of our life, and save her that is grieved in spirit speedily, even in our days. Praised art Thou, O Lord, Who makest Zion joyful through her children.

The significance of this poetic imagery is that neither the prophets nor the Rabbis considered "Mother Jerusalem" as a spiritual entity that existed either in heaven or only in the mystic visions of an apocalyptic cosmology. Jerusalem or "Mother Zion" always represented a geographic entity, and the "daughter of Jerusalem" was always the people of Israel. This is not to say that the concept of a heavenly Jerusalem did not exist in rabbinic thought. But it was not rooted in Jewish thinking, and it remained a mere, vague shadow of the real Jerusalem.

This, of course, is the reverse of the Christian concept of the heavenly Jerusalem. In Christian theology, the heavenly Jerusalem is the dominant concept, and terrestrial Jerusalem is merely a city where holy places exist. In Christian liturgy, the mystic vision of a spiritual Jerusalem predominates; in Jewish liturgy, Jerusalem, the earthly city of David, the hope of rebuilding the sanctuary on the Temple Mount, and the physical ingathering of the Jewish exiles, constitute the central concerns of Jewish worship. These liturgical concepts are the authentic expressions of Judaism, and in them, one can find the answer to the seeming mystery of the Jewish attachment to Jerusalem. For the Jew, Jerusalem is not merely a place where holy events once took place. The city is holy not only because the Holy Temple once stood there. Jerusalem is central in Jewish thought because the city itself is everlastingly holy and is forever the center of Jewish hope. Jerusalem is holy because it was the city of David, wherein stood the central shrine of divine worship, and, equally important, Jerusalem is still the center of the people of Israel. In messianic days, Jerusalem will again harbor the central shrine of Judaism. That is why Jews rejected the British offer of Uganda for the establishment of a Jewish state. That is why the Russian offer of Birobidzhan evoked no positive response among Russian Jews. The offer of Uganda was rejected and the offer of Birobidzhan just faded out of existence. The Jewish bond to Jerusalem is eternal.

Jerusalem in the Christian Tradition

Christian orientation has traditionally been away from the national to the universal and from the terrestrial to the heavenly dimensions of faith. Hence, Jerusalem became increasingly a heavenly concept. In the New Testament, one finds this concept clearly stated:

> Then came one of the seven angels . . . and showed me the holy city Jerusalem, coming down out of heaven from God, having the glory of God, its radiance like a most rare jewel . . . (Rev. 21:9–11).[4]

This mystic view of Jerusalem penetrated Christian thinking and at times dominated Christian theology. Accordingly, many leading Christians saw in terrestrial Jerusalem a mere transitory phenomenon, ephemeral and inconsequential in the religious experience of the faithful. Indeed, Jerusalem has often been equated with the Church and also with any place where the faithful live a Christian life.

This mystic concept of the heavenly Jerusalem introduced an element of ambiguity into the Christian attitude to the city of Jerusalem. While the heavenly Jerusalem was the goal of the spiritual aspirations of the pious, the earthly Jerusalem continued to be a place of sacred associations and stirring memories. Whereas the heavenly Jerusalem was in the center of Christian piety and theology, it never blotted out the natural veneration of the sites that were directly associated with the formative years of Christianity. Terrestrial Jerusalem was revered because it was there that Jesus preached his doctrines; it was there that he consummated his ministry in his passion on the cross; it was there that he was buried; and it was there that the miracle of his

---

4. See also Gal. 4:26, Hebr. 12:22, Rev. 3:12, and other references in the New Testament.

resurrection took place. Jerusalem is therefore the cradle of Christianity, and the most sacred monuments of early Christianity are located there.

Notwithstanding the spiritualization of Jerusalem, popular piety has clung to the earthly Jerusalem as a holy city where the Christian can visit the holy sites which are considered efficacious for prayer. In addition, the pious Christian wants to reexperience the momentous events of the birth of Christianity by reenacting the stirring moments of Jesus' last days on earth. The Church has encouraged pilgrimages to Jerusalem because visiting the holy places tends to awaken, in the heart of the pilgrim, sacred emotions and tends to strengthen and deepen his faith. The Church has, therefore, been concerned for free access to the holy places, for their protection against desecration, and for the maintenance of peaceful conditions to enable the devout Christian pilgrims to come and pray in peace. Any government that can guarantee these conditions is theoretically acceptable to the Christian communities.

A mighty Christian outburst of enthusiasm for Jerusalem erupted at the end of the eleventh century. The main source of this enthusiasm was largely a reaction to Moslem interference with the free flow of Christian pilgrims to Jerusalem's holy places. The Crusaders' rallying cry was to capture the Holy Sepulchre and to free it from the hands of the infidels. To be sure, there were also other motives, some not so spiritual, that attracted men to the Crusaders' ranks. But these are irrelevant to the theme at hand. This remarkable outburst of religious ferment led to the conquest of Jerusalem and the establishment of a Christian political state. But the Crusaders, during their short interlude, did not establish a firm political state. They built convents, churches, and fortresses, but they remained sojourners who came to rescue the Christian shrines. Their eyes and hearts were turned westward to their homes and families. Their coming was only for the purpose of ensuring free access to the holy places, to guarantee the freedom of worship, and to safeguard the holy sites from desecration by the infidels.

The Christian concern for the holy places has led the Vatican to support the United Nations plan to internationalize Jerusalem. Within such an arrangement, the safety of the holy sites would be assured. Neither Jews nor Moslems would control Jerusalem. The Church would have a greater influence in the city's government and in the maintenance of the holy places. Lately, the Vatican has been less insistent on internationalization, and has asked for a special status for the holy places. But this vague expression does not cancel the former explicit demand for internationalization. However, what is actually best for Jerusalem and for the holy places is not internationalization, which can only bring intrigue and instability.

Jerusalem in the Islamic Tradition

Muhammad, the founder of Islam, took many of his basic concepts from the Jews and Christians. Among these was the sanctity of Jerusalem. The city is not specifically mentioned in the Koran. However, Moslem scholars say that Jerusalem is implied in one of the passages of the Koran. More explicit is Muhammad's instruction that his followers should face, during prayer, in the direction of Jerusalem, as Jews have been doing to this day. Some claim that this was part of Muhammad's strategy which aimed at winning over the Jewish tribes of the Arabian Peninsula. It was only when he failed to win the Jews over that he changed the direction of prayer to Mecca. But the sanctity of Jerusalem did not vanish from Islam when it broke with both Judaism and Christianity.

Moslem theologians derive Jerusalem's sanctity from the events which, they claim, took place during the days of the prophet. To begin with, they quote the verse from the Koran:

> Glory be to Him, Who carried His servant by night from the Holy Mosque to the Further Mosque, the precincts which We have blessed, that We might show him some of Our signs (Koran 17:1).

This verse may have only referred to Muhammad's consecration to his prophetic mission. However, the verse has been interpreted, in Islam, as referring to the sanctity of Jerusalem. The "Further Mosque," they say, means Jerusalem, or more specifically the Temple Mount, which Moslems call the *Haram al-Sharif*. Whatever was the original meaning of the "Further Mosque," among Moslems it refers to Jerusalem and is taken as definitive proof of Jerusalem's holiness in Islam.

More important has been the oral but authoritative tradition according to which Muhammad had made a miraculous nocturnal journey from Mecca to Jerusalem, and from there ascended to heaven. He made his journey to Jerusalem on his miraculous steed, Buraq. This extraordinary steed was tethered to the inside of the Western Wall of the Temple Mount. Moslems, therefore, regard the Wall as a Moslem holy place. The angel Gabriel accompanied him on this celestial journey, where Muhammad met many of the biblical personages from Abraham to Jesus; he saw both paradise and hell; and he learned, from God's mouth, the teachings which are incorporated in the Koran. This miraculous tale has become an article of faith in Islam.

The miracle of Muhammad's ascent to heaven was later elaborated and definitive proof was added, such as grooves showing Muhammad's footprints on the Rock. In time to come, the final judgment would take place in Jerusalem. Thus, Jerusalem's sanctity in Islam was firmly and permanently established. To commemorate these sacred events in the formative days of Islam, a special annual feast was fixed in the Moslem calendar.

After the Prophet's death, the Moslems began their ever-widening conquests, and Jerusalem fell to their victorious armies in the year 638. Jerusalem ceased to be a far-off city; it was now within the Moslem territories. The tradition of Jerusalem's sanctity now ceased to be a mere abstract tradition; it became a concrete reality.

The Caliph Omar, who conquered Jerusalem, had the Temple Mount cleaned of the dung that the Christians had deposited there to show their contempt for the Jews and Judaism. Sixty years after Omar's conquest of Jerusalem, the Caliph Abd-al-Malik erected the magnificent Dome of the Rock. Shortly thereafter, the Al-Aqsa Mosque was built in the southern part of the Haram. While the Dome was designed as a shrine for the glorification of the Holy Rock, the Al-Aqsa Mosque was intended to be a house of public prayer. These shrines enhanced the sanctity of Jerusalem in Islam. In Moslem literature, Jerusalem's praise has been exalted in an authoritative dictum stating that five prayers in Jerusalem will cleanse the pilgrim and he shall be as pure as on the day of his birth. Since five prayers are the total of a day's worship, this maxim promises total purification of sin in exchange for one day's pilgrimage to Jerusalem. How can a faithful Moslem resist such an advantageous deal? But the pilgrimage to Jerusalem was to be made only after the faithful had made his pilgrimage to Mecca and Medina, for Jerusalem is, in Islam, only the third of the holy cities.

Many historians have been perplexed by the contradiction between the Moslem veneration of Jerusalem and their shabby treatment of the city. Throughout the centuries of Moslem rule in Jerusalem, the city was relegated to the status of a provincial town, never rising even to the rank of a provincial capital. During these centuries, Jerusalem remained a neglected and decaying city, distinguished by its ruins rather than its habitations. Only three relatively brief periods were noted for their building activity in the city: (1) After Omar's conquest of the city, the Dome of the Rock and the Al-Aqsa Mosque were erected; (2) during the Mameluke period, there was a spate of building activity that left its mark on the city's appearance; and (3) under Suleiman the Magnificent, the city walls were rebuilt.

As was the case after the Crusaders' capture of Jerusalem, when the city's sanctity was made the goal of a Moslem holy war on the Christian infidels, so after the Six-Day War, Jerusalem's sanctity in Islam has received increased emphasis. In Islam, religion, and politics are inextricable from each other. Religious and political forces are, therefore, jointly engaged in the stubborn struggle for Jerusalem. For Israel, this is a life and death struggle. For the Arabs, this principle of *Dar al-Islam*—the inviolability of the "realm of the faithful"—involves the political control of places wherein Islamic holy sites are located. It is therefore the holy sites in Jerusalem that attaches the Moslem to the city. The Moslem claim to Jerusalem is thus a corollary to the location of the sacred sites on the Temple Mount.

The Riddle of Jerusalem's Survival and Rebirth

Jerusalem is one of the world's miracles. The city's glory went into exile together with the Jews almost two thousand years ago, and the city became a mere provincial town. Under Byzantine rule, Caesarea was the capital of Palestine; under the Moslems, Ramle became the capital of the land; under the Mamelukes, Gaza was the seat of government; under the Turks, Damascus was the pasha's headquarters; and when the Old City returned to Arab rule from

1948 to 1967, Amman was the seat of government. Jerusalem became the capital of the mandated territory under the British in 1918, and, in 1949, part of the city rose to the status of capital of the State of Israel. Finally, in 1967, united Jerusalem once more rose to the position it had occupied in ancient times, in the days of King David, King Solomon, and in the days of the prophets Isaiah and Jeremiah. This is truly a tale of resurrection from oblivion to grandeur and from degradation to dignity.

The religious communities of Jerusalem are now free to worship at their shrines and holy places in dignity and security. As a focus of international religious concern, Jerusalem has experienced a reawakening, and its spiritual influence promises to grow and have a beneficial impact on the devotees of the three faiths for which Jerusalem is holy.

1

Jerusalem's Early History

Jerusalem is one of a string of towns along the central ridge of the Holy Land. Among the better known of these towns are Nablus to the north and Hebron to the south. Jerusalem's location was determined by two factors which were in ancient times definitive considerations: the availability of water and the defensibility of the site. The site where Jerusalem is located is blessed with a natural spring in its immediate vicinity. The perennial spring, called Gihon, was the only source of water within a radius of three miles. This spring insured the city with an uninterrupted, though scanty, supply of water.

The site of ancient Jerusalem was also blessed with excellent defensive potentialities. It was located on the southern hill slope of Mount Moriah. This site is now outside the southern city wall, and is a hill known as the Ophel. It extends, along a narrow area, to the Gihon Spring. This location on the Ophel is surrounded on three sides by deep ravines. The Kidron Valley is on the east, the

Hinnom Valley on the south, and the Tyropean Valley on the west. In later times, the city expanded westward and included what is now called Mount Zion. Only the northern side of the town needed extensive fortification. Throughout Jerusalem's history, enemies preferred to attack the city from the vulnerable northern side. When we read in Jeremiah: "Out of the north the evil shall break forth" (Jer. 1:14), the prophet spoke not only of a specific enemy to the north of Judah, but also of the usual approach of enemies who sought to conquer Jerusalem.

Jerusalem's name is no longer a matter of conjecture. One can declare with a sense of certainty that the name Jerusalem is very ancient, predating by centuries the arrival of the Israelites. The days of speculation ended when archeologists unearthed cuneiform documents in which the city is called Uru-Salem. *Uru* is an old derivative of the word for city, and *Salem* was the name of a local deity. Hence the name of the city was originally the City of the god Salem. When the Hebrews entered the land, they associated the word *Salem* with *Shalom*, the Hebrew word for peace. Thus Jerusalem became the City of Peace, and Psalm 122 is dedicated to the theme of "the peace of Jerusalem":

Pray for the peace of Jerusalem.
May they prosper that love thee.
Peace be within thy walls
and prosperity within thy palaces (Ps. 122:6–7).

When the Jebusites occupied the city, it assumed an additional appellation, derived from the name of the people who lived in it at the time. The city was called Jebus. With the defeat of the Jebusites by King David, the city reverted to its original historic name of Jerusalem. One cannot assign exact dates to these events. However, the sequence of these events is quite clear and helpful in tracing the development of the city's name.

In the early tradition of Israel, Jerusalem is not a Hebrew holy city. Archeologists have not found, in the strata corresponding to the early biblical period, evidence of any cultic role played by Jerusalem. Indeed, the major holy cities for the Israelites were then Shilo, Beth El, Shechem, and several other places, but not Jerusalem. The Samaritan claim that Mount Gerizim was a holy mountain should not be dismissed out of hand. Where the Samaritan's claim is deficient is in its confusion of origin with substance or genesis with function. The preeminence of a holy place is not determined by its age. The fact is that Jerusalem became and has remained the sacred city of Judaism and its derivative religions of Christianity and Islam.

When Joshua entered the land of Canaan, he apparently did not capture the city. It was too strongly fortified. It demanded too much time and sophisticated implements of war, neither of which Joshua had. Besides, he had to meet more urgent challenges from alliances of local rulers. When Joshua divided the conquered land among the tribes, the boundary of Judah ran south of the Jebusites (Josh. 15:8). Thus, the city was left theoretically to the portion of Benjamin. But it was the tribe of Judah that attempted its capture. However, in Joshua's day, the city was still able to resist the Israelite invaders, and it was strong enough to negotiate a peace treaty as we read in the Bible:

> But the Jebusites, the inhabitants of Jerusalem, the people of Judah could not drive out; so the Jebusites dwell with the people of Judah at Jerusalem to this day. (Josh. 15:63).

During the years that followed Joshua's conquest of the land, the moral and spiritual character of the people sank to a low state. The martial spirit of the people also degenerated. Instead of being a nation feared by the inhabitants of the area, they were frequently subject to the surrounding peoples. And the city of Jerusalem continued as an independent enclave, defiant of the Israelites who lived round about. The Jebusites thus remained in possession of Jerusalem, secure in their fortress which nature had provided with superb advantages.

The state of national decline was stemmed by the great Samuel, whom the Bible places only second to Moses in spiritual stature. Samuel led the Israelites out of their degenerate idolatry, aroused their martial spirit, and partly brought back their lost glory. He succeeded in inspiring the people with a new hope and a new vision and, above all, awakened in them a new spirit of self-confidence and a revived faith in their God. This led to a political revolution—the founding of a monarchical government. The first king, Saul, succeeded in uniting the people against the common enemy, the Philistines. But tribal jealousies and intrigues, real or imaginary, undermined the king's moral fibre and his capability to rule effectively. It was during the reign of King Saul's successor that the nation's unity was finally achieved; and that, for only a relatively short time.

When King Saul fell in battle against the Philistines, the tribes rallied around David and crowned him king. In David, the people had a great leader who was destined not only to defeat their enemies, but to unite them as a nation. The most important factor in this process of nation building was David's decision to capture Jerusalem from the Jebusites.

David recognized the city's advantages. It was almost impregnable. For centuries it had defied all invaders. One of David's first tasks was, therefore, the conquest of this foreign enclave within his kingdom. When David's men laid siege to the city, the Jebusites taunted and mocked them, saying: "Except thou take away the blind and the lame, thou shalt not come in hither" (2 Sam. 5:6). David's men, however, did manage to come into the city. Joab, King David's leading warrior, and a number of his men discovered a shaft that connected the city with its source of water. Using this shaft they were able to infiltrate under the walls and taking the city by surprise.

David also recognized the city's political preeminence. Not only was Jerusalem centrally located, but it was situated in neutral territory. It was neither within the territory of his own tribe of Judah, nor within Ephraim, the leading tribe of the north. To be sure, the city was very close to his own tribe of Judah. It was on the very borderline. Technically, the city was within the territory of the smaller tribe of Benjamin. However, David, having taken the city with his personal troops, declared the city as his personal property, calling it the City of David—that is, neutral territory belonging to none of the tribes. The selection of Jerusalem as the new capital would thus calm intertribal jealousies, and help in the creation of a united nation, much as the creation of the District of Columbia for the siting of the capital of the United States calmed the potential rivalry and jealousy of the several states. David, therefore, moved the seat of his government from Hebron to Jerusalem. He also strengthened the city's fortifications, enclosing both the upper and lower parts of the city within the walls. The city's wall crossed the intervening valley between the two parts of the city over a landfill or an artificial embankment, referred to in the Bible as the *Millo*. Jerusalem thus became, for the first time, the capital of an empire.

Of greater importance was David's decision to make Jerusalem the religious center of the nation. He transferred to Jerusalem the Ark of the Covenant, which contained the Tablets on which were inscribed the Ten Commandments. This supreme emblem of God's presence among the people had not found a permanent resting place ever since the Israelites crossed the Jordan under Joshua. David and the elders of Israel now brought the Ark to Jerusalem "with joy." Jerusalem thus became both the capital and the place which God had chosen "to put His name there" (Deut. 12:21). To be sure, it was not the sole place of divine worship. There were several rival sacred cities, some with superior credentials of sanctity, such as Beth-El, Hebron, and Shechem. But Jerusalem's star as the holy city was rising and was destined to become the sole and practically unrivalled place wherein dwelled God's presence and wherein the nation worshipped the God of their fathers. The city was now called the City of David because it was he who endowed it with temporal and spiritual preeminence.

It was David's intention to build "a house for the Lord," a fitting sanctuary to house the Holy Ark. The sanctuary was to be located on Mount Moriah where, according to tradition, the sacrifice of Isaac had taken place. Therefore, David purchased the threshing floor on Mount Moriah from its owner, Araunah the Jebusite, and he built there an altar. He also made plans for the erection of a temple, and he gathered building material for the structure. However, he was not destined to carry out his intentions. Nonetheless, David's success dwarfed his anticipations and exceeded even his wildest dreams. Jerusalem became, for all time, the Holy City of Israel. And when the state ceased to exist, and the Jews were scattered to the four corners of the earth, Jerusalem continued to live in their hearts and consciousness.

According to the Bible, King David was buried in the City of David; that is, somewhere to the south of the Temple Mount. However, David's traditional burial place is on what is now called Mount Zion and has become a holy place revered by Jews, Christians, and Moslems.

When Solomon, David's son, ascended the throne, he resolved to finish what his father had begun, and he erected the Temple which has ever since been called by his name. The Temple which he erected stood on Mount

Moriah, near where the Dome of the Rock is now located. Substructures were built into the native rock for cisterns to hold the water needed for the ritual ablutions, and drains were fashioned for carrying away the refuse of the sacrificial rites. Some of these substructures have survived to this day.

The Temple structure itself contained a windowless room known as the Holy of Holies. In this most holy chamber rested the Ark which contained the Tablets of the Ten Commandments. Only the high priest (*Kohen Gadol*) entered this most sacred chamber, and only once annually on the Day of Atonement. In synagogues today, the Holy of Holies of the Temple is symbolized by an Ark which contains the scrolls of the Torah. In front of this Ark, there is a curtain, as was formerly in the Temple.

Another chamber next to the Holy of Holies contained, among other ritual objects, the altar of incense and the Table of Shewbread. This chamber was larger than the Holy of Holies and was accessible to all members of the priestly caste. Outside this holy chamber, there was an extensive court that was open to all Israelites. The altar of burnt offerings was located in this court.

The Temple was a most impressive structure. Yet it was not original in conception. It followed the plan of the tabernacle that had been built in the wilderness in the days of Moses. Obviously, it was larger, but not of immense size. Its fame rested on the splendor of its architecture and on its exquisite ornamentation. No building, sacred or secular, has ever received such generous praise in its own day and in ages after. Its remembrance has persisted with reverence and yearning to this day. Even when the Temple was destroyed, the site of the Temple and of the city of Jerusalem remained the national and religious center of the Jewish people. Thousands of years have not dimmed the hope, and interminable exile and persecution have not diluted the faith of the Jew in Jerusalem's restoration.

Solomon was a great builder. He also erected for himself and his household a magnificent palace; he enlarged the walls of the city to embrace the Temple Mount; and he built the immense cisterns near Bethlehem, known as Solomon's Pools, to provide the city with water. In order to bring the water to Jerusalem, he built a vast system of conduits and aqueducts. On the Temple Mount, he constructed reservoirs for storing the water from the pools as well as the water from the annual winter rainfalls.

Solomon's fame as a wise and resourceful king spread far and wide. But his fame was tarnished by his large harem, around which political treaties were concluded and domestic intrigues hatched. While Solomon's harem helped maintain peace with neighboring potentates, it also corroded the moral foundations of the state. The princesses he married brought their idolatries with them. Solomon tolerated their idolatrous worship. For this, Solomon was harshly condemned.

While Solomon's sins have not been forgotten, his achievements, especially the construction of the Temple on Mount Moriah, have been remembered, and his memory has been counted for a blessing by innumerable generations of Jews, Christians, and Moslems.

2

From the Partition of David's Empire to the City's Fall in 586 B.C.E.

King Solomon was succeeded by his son Rehoboam. No sooner did the new king ascend the throne than he was faced with a revolt that led to the partition of his kingdom. David's empire was thus reduced to two relatively weak kingdoms. The northern kingdom, known as Israel, was by far the larger and stronger; the southern kingdom, known as Judah, was the smaller and weaker. But the southern kingdom was more stable. The dynasty established by King David continued to rule in Jerusalem for over four hundred years, up to the time when the land was conquered by the Babylonians in the year 586 B.C.E. The northern kingdom, however, was marked by governmental instability and survived only about 250 years. In 721 B.C.E., the Assyrians overran the Kingdom of Israel and the population was exiled. The inhabitants of the northern kingdom, often referred to as the Ten Tribes of Israel, were largely assimi-

lated into the population of the lands of their exile.[1] The
survival of the Kingdom of Judah for an additional century
and a half accounts, in large measure, for the survival of
the Jewish nation.

The difference in the survival potential of the two Hebrew nations is to be found mainly in the rise of a line of
remarkable spiritual giants who taught the word of God
with courage and personal example. The prophets were not
always listened to, let alone followed, but they always
stirred the people's conscience, as is implied by the words
of one of these prophets:

> And Thou shalt say unto them:
> Thus saith the Lord God.
> And they, whether they will hear,
>   or whether they will forbear . . .
> Yet shall they know that there hath
>   been a prophet among them (Ezek. 2:4–5).

Four centuries intervened between the reign of King
Solomon and the fall of Judah. During that period, Jerusalem saw years of glory and years of disaster. Jerusalem
experienced sieges by foreign armies and several severe
earthquakes. Years of disaster were followed by years of
deliverance, and periods of spiritual decline were followed
by periods of moral rectitude. Kings ruled and prophets
preached the word of God. Corruption and spiritual awak-
ening often confronted each other, bringing in their wake
either moral decline or spiritual regeneration.

During those centuries, the city of Jerusalem also underwent physical changes that altered the city's topography.

---

1. The small Samaritan sect, numbering about 500 souls, claims to
be the remnant of the ancient Israelites. But even if that claim is
accepted as historic fact, it can hardly be considered a real national
survival.

The city of David slowly moved northwestward, up the hill to the present location of the Old City. By the seventh century B.C.E., during the reign of King Hezekiah, the western boundary of the city was on the hill above the central valley, which was later called the Tyropean Valley.

During the reign of King Hezekiah (724–695 B.C.E.) extensive building activities were initiated. They were aimed at strengthening the city against the threat of an Assyrian attack. Among King Hezekiah's most enduring works was the construction of a tunnel from the Gihon Spring outside the city wall to the Siloam Pool, which was inside the city fortifications. An inscription commemorating the successful completion of this ambitious engineering feat was discovered in the tunnel and is now on view at the Istanbul Museum. The Temple Mount was above the ancient City of David, but it was somewhat below the new residential section known as the Upper City. However, the people of Jerusalem continued to "go up" to the Temple when, actually, those who lived in the Upper City were going down to it.

The many sieges, earthquakes, and destructions partially filled in the valleys with the debris of the city's destroyed walls and houses. In addition, the winds and rains helped the filling process. To be sure, Jerusalem continued to be surrounded on three sides by deep ravines, but these ravines were no longer as deep as they had been in the days of King David.

The prophets now concentrated their prophetic teachings on Jerusalem. Isaiah and Jeremiah both prophesied in Jerusalem and their message has come down the ages as "the word of God in Jerusalem." The prophets attacked idolatry, injustice, and hypocrisy. The centrality of Jerusalem as God's chosen city received increased emphasis.

During the period which intervened between the fall of Israel in 721 B.C.E. and the fall of Judah in 586 B.C.E., an event of transcendent importance transpired in the land of

Judah. The event was inspired by the prophets, and its outcome was Jerusalem's rise to the status of the sole sacred city in the land. Although the Jerusalem shrine had overshadowed all other sanctuaries in the land, the other sanctuaries continued to function, and some of them thrived and exerted considerable influence in their localities. Some of these shrines traced their origin to the patriarchs. There were also many "high places" where the idolatries of the Canaanites survived and even flourished. The prophets vigorously and incessantly protested against these local sanctuaries. After centuries of prophetic opposition to the idolatrous shrines, a violent cultural revolution erupted. It occurred during the reign of King Josiah (638–607 B.C.E.). All the local sanctuaries and "high places" were demolished and the Jerusalem Temple became the only shrine in the land of Judah. Jerusalem thus became the sole and supreme holy city of the Jews.

As time went on, the prophetic words sank more deeply into the conscience of the Judeans. When the sad day arrived and Jerusalem was captured by the Babylonians in the year 586 B.C.E., the Temple was burned to the ground, and the exiles wept for the fate that befell their capital and holy city.

> How lonely sits the city
>   that was full of people!
> How like a widow has she become,
>   she that was great among the nations!
> She that was a princess among the cities
>   has become a vassal (Lam. 1:1).

The destruction of the Temple was then as tragic for the Jews as their exile from their land. The Temple was more than a center of worship; it was the Jew's means of access to his God. It was only in the Temple that the Jew could achieve an interrelationship with God. Since the Temple ritual could be effective only if performed at the sacred location specifically chosen by God, the Temple ritual had to cease, and the Jew found himself cut off from God. He was thus exiled both physically and spiritually, and the spiritual exile was probably the more tragic because the Jew no longer had hope of redemption from sin. The words of the Book of Lamentations can only be understood in the framework of this dual tragedy that engulfed the Jews.

3

From the Babylonian Captivity to the Hasmonean Victory

The Judean exiles in Babylonia did not assimilate as is usual with conquered and exiled peoples. Their attachment to Jerusalem and to their faith was resolute and unyielding. It was dramatically expressed by the psalmist's oath: "If I forget thee, O Jerusalem, let my right hand forget her cunning" (Ps. 137:5). The Jews saw in the disaster a vindication of the prophets and their warnings. The continued presence of prophets in their midst was an additional factor in their survival as a distinctive people. While the prophets in Jerusalem emphasized the coming disaster as an inevitable consequence of the people's faithlessness to God and His teachings, the prophets of the exile spoke words of comfort and hope. The Jews had paid for their transgressions and God would soon send redemption and healing. The spirit of the exiles was sustained and their spiritual vitality remained undiminished. They even succeeded in evolving a new religious institution to fill the vacuum created by the suspension of the Temple ritual.

This new institution, known as the synagogue, ushered in a new form of divine worship in which study and prayer took the place of the sacrificial rites of the Temple. The synagogue was destined to be more than a makeshift solution. It became a permanent institution in Judaism, and later, when the Second Temple was erected, the synagogue coexisted with it. For thousands of years the synagogue has continued to be a powerful force in the spiritual and intellectual life of the Jewish people. In time, it also became the prototype of the Christian church and the Moslem mosque.

The prophetic words of comfort were fulfilled. Within half a century of the fall of Jerusalem, the Babylonian empire fell. Cyrus, king of Persia, overthrew the Babylonian empire in 537 B.C.E. and issued a declaration permitting the Jewish exiles to return to the Holy Land and to rebuild their Temple in Jerusalem. Only a relatively small number, about 40,000, uprooted themselves and returned to Jerusalem. They found the city desolate and the neighboring people hostile. After years of discouragement and frustration, due largely to the fierce opposition from the neighboring population, the Jews succeeded in erecting the second Temple on the spot where Solomon's Temple had stood.

In the year of 516 B.C.E., seventy years after the destruction of Solomon's Temple by the Babylonians, the new Temple was dedicated with great rejoicing. The new Temple was built to the same dimensions as the first Temple. However, it lacked its lustre. The biblical account relates that there were old men who still remembered Solomon's Temple. When they saw the new structure that was being consecrated, they compared it with the grandeur of the first Temple and wept. However, more important than the lack of the embellishments of the first Temple was the lack of the Ark of the Covenant, which contained the Tablets of the Ten Commandments. When Jerusalem was sacked by the Babylonians in 586 B.C.E., the Ark of the Covenant was lost and never recovered. In the new Temple, the Holy of Holies remained empty. To this day there are those who speculate about the whereabouts of the Ark. Some have claimed that the Ark was hidden somewhere in the Temple compound and that its hiding place will be revealed when the Messiah comes. That, of course, will be "at the end of days." However, the Temple ritual was resumed, and Jerusalem was again the religious center of the Jews.

About half a century later, the Jewish community of Jerusalem was reinforced by a new wave of immigrants from Babylonia. This group contained two leaders, Ezra and Nehemiah, men of great spiritual statue. Ezra revived the spiritual life of the people; Nehemiah strengthened the civic and political fabric of the community. Among Nehemiah's significant deeds was his rebuilding of the city's wall. The new wall was erected on the old foundations, which accounts for its rapid completion. The new wall gave the inhabitants the protection they sorely needed. No longer were they exposed to attacks and plunder. They now had the peace they needed for the practice and development of their unique religious life. The high priests headed the government, and a harmonious, peaceful, and religious life characterized Jerusalem's Jewish society. The city's spiritual influence was evident for the first time in a Jewish diaspora, especially in Babylonia.

This peaceful state continued throughout the Persian hegemony. It was finally disturbed by the entry of the Hellenistic culture, which followed the conquests of Alexander the Great. Jerusalem's era of peace and quietude was seriously shaken, and a new era of stress and conflict was initiated. The effects of this tension on the Jewish people, and indeed on a large segment of humanity, were far-reaching.

Alexander defeated King Darius in the battle of Issus. He then subdued the neighboring provinces. After the fall of the maritime cities of Tyre and Gaza, in 331 B.C.E., Alexander led his forces against Jerusalem. Josephus' account of this historic event is as follows: When Alexander came within three miles of Jerusalem, he was met by a procession of the people, headed by the Jerusalem priests dressed in their white linen garments and the high priest resplendent in his priestly robes. Alexander dismounted and knelt before the high priest. Alexander explained his strange behavior by relating a dream in which he saw a divine being who foretold his victories. That divine being he recognized in the face of the high priest.

Be that as it may, the city was spared and peace continued to reign in Jerusalem. However, a new and more dangerous challenge was now introduced into the life of Jerusalem. Alexander brought with him not only a conquering army, but a new culture which challenged and threatened the religious foundations of Judaism. Alexander's army did not enter Jerusalem, but the Hellenistic culture which followed his conquests penetrated deeply into the life of Jerusalem's inhabitants. The upper classes, in particular, led in the process of assimilation to Hellenistic culture. A gymnasium in the Greek fashion was built near the Temple and, at the northwestern corner of the Temple Mount, a fortress—the Acra—was erected. This fortress remained the stronghold of the Hellenistic elements, both Jewish and foreign, till its fall in 142 B.C.E. In the process of Hellenization, the gymnasium occupied an important place, for athletic games were played not only for physical exercise but also in honor of the pagan gods. By the end of the second century B.C.E., some of the younger functionaries of the Temple would rush from the Temple rituals to the gymnasium to participate in the Hellenic games. This shocked the Jewish conservative elements. The degeneration that had set in undermined even the high priesthood, whose offices had become political plums, often purchased from the government by the highest bidders.

When Antiochus IV ascended the throne in 175 B.C.E., he initiated a policy that aimed at stamping out Judaism. It is speculated that he wanted Jerusalem and the whole land of Israel to be part of his Hellenistic empire, not only politically but also culturally. This policy, he hoped, would strengthen his realm against the Egyptians. An "Antioch in Jerusalem" was to be established, with the Temple turned into a pagan shrine. The Greek gods were henceforth to be worshipped in the Jerusalem Temple, and swine were to be the daily offerings on the altar. The reading and study of the Torah were strictly forbidden, as were other fundamental practices of Judaism. Apostacy was vigorously promoted.

At this state of degradation, deliverance came through a violent revolt led by a priestly family, the Hasmoneans. The leaders of that revolt were Mattathias and his five sons. The revolt began in Modiin, a town located about eighteen miles to the west of Jerusalem. The battles were brilliantly led by one of the brothers, Judah Maccabeus. He initially engaged the foe in what is now called guerrilla warfare. Success led to the engagement of the enemy in formal battles. The oppressor was ousted from the land; the Temple was cleansed of its defilements; and the traditional rites were resumed with great rejoicing. To this day the Jews celebrate the annual Feast of Lights or Hanukkah in commemoration of that event.

But Jerusalem remained divided between the Jews and their adversaries. For seventeen years, the Temple Mount and the Lower City to the south were in the hands of the Hasmoneans, while the Upper City and the Acra fortress at the northwest corner of the Temple Mount were in the hands of the Hellenists and the Syrian troops. In 142 B.C.E., Simon, the last of the five Hasmonean brothers, captured the Acra. Jerusalem was finally united and thereafter served as the capital of the Hasmonean kingdom. During this period of prosperity, new walls were erected around the city.

The descendants of the Hasmonean family ruled in Jerusalem for about a century. Power, however, tends to breed demoralization, and the Hasmonean kings were hardly the exception to this rule. As a result of an inner dissension between two brothers in the matter of succession, Rome stepped in. The Hasmonean dynasty was thus extinguished, and Roman rule, through vassal kings and Roman procurators, began.

4

The Reign
of Herod the Great

In the year 63 B.C.E., two Hasmonean brothers who dis-
puted their respective claims to the throne called on Rome
to mediate and decide the issue. This proved to be the
immediate cause that brought Rome, the rising superpower of that age, into the land of Israel. When Rome's
mediation was rejected, Pompey invaded the land and laid
siege to Jerusalem. He took advantage of the Jewish refusal
to enter battle on the Sabbath, and thus achieved an easy
victory. He breached the wall, captured the city, forced his
way into the Temple, and entered the Holy of Holies. One
can readily imagine his surprise. He had expected to find
some impressive representation of the Jewish deity. Instead he found a dark, windowless, empty room!

From that day on, the Holy Land, which had been ruled
by the Hasmonean dynasty for a century, became virtually
a Roman colony. Pompey installed one of the Hasmoneans
as ruler. However, after some Jewish insurrections against
the Roman puppets, Rome chose a new ruler, a person

named Herod. In 37 B.C.E., Herod overthrew the last
Hasmonean king and, with the help of Rome, ascended the
throne. His ascent to the throne is described by Harry
Emerson Fosdick in these striking words:

> Herod the Great, who, as another said, stole to his throne
> like a fox, ruled like a tiger, and died like a dog, had seized
> Jerusalem with a Roman army in 37 B.C., in a victory so
> murderous that he himself asked the Romans whether they
> purposed making him king of a desert.[1]

Herod was a complex personality. He was the grandson
of an Idumean who had converted to Judaism, and his
father had been an important official in the court of the
last Hasmonean king. Herod yearned for the people's
acceptance as the legitimate successor to the Hasmonean
throne. But the Jews held him in contempt. To them, he
was an Idumean traitor, a Roman lackey, and a bloodthirsty tyrant. He was all that, but not an Idumean except
for his descent. Archeological evidence seems to indicate
that, in matters of ritual observance, he was fully a Jew. He
strictly observed the minutiae of Jewish religious ritual.
Still, he was hated, and he responded with bitterness and
cruelty. He brought peace to the land and fame to Jerusalem, but he received in return only grudging obedience due
solely to fear of dreadful reprisals.

Herod is remembered primarily for his magnificent
structures. Archeologists have unearthed many Herodian
relics of historic importance. Among them are relics of
palaces, temples, amphitheaters, fortresses, and hippo-
dromes which he erected, mostly in honor of his Roman
patrons. In Jerusalem he built, in addition to the new
Temple, a magnificent palace which was situated near the

---

1. Harry Emerson Fosdick, *A Pilgrimage to Palestine* (New York:
Macmillan Publishing Co., 1949), p. 186.

present Jaffa Gate. Between the palace and the Jaffa Gate, he constructed three strong towers named *Phasael*, *Hippicus*, and *Miriamne*. Some of the masonry of the Phasael Tower can still be seen in the lower part of what is now called the Tower of David. King David, of course, had no connection with this structure.

Herod also rebuilt the fortress at the northwest corner of the Temple compound, and he renamed it *Antonia* in honor of Mark Anthony. Christian tradition locates the trial of Jesus at the Antonia fortress. Hence, the First Station of the Cross on the Via Dolorosa is on the site of that fortress. Herod also built a second wall on the northern side of the city. The exact location of this wall has been a subject of many disputes. On the exact location of that wall depends the authenticity of no less a shrine than the Holy Sepulchre.

Another of Herod's structures in Jerusalem is what is now called Wilson's Arch. This Arch is located in the northern section of the Wailing Wall and is in a perfect state of preservation. In Herod's day, it supported a bridge which connected the Temple Mount with the Upper City. Another Arch, a remnant of which is known as Robinson's Arch, has not been preserved. Only a remnant of its support is to be seen on the Western Wall of the Temple compound, somewhat to the south of the Wailing Wall. This Arch supported a staircase which led down from the Temple Mount to the Tyropean Valley below.

The pride of Herod's building enterprises was the reconstruction of the second Temple, which had been erected in 516 B.C.E., soon after the return from Babylonia. That Temple had served the religious needs of the Jews for almost 500 years. Although this Temple was of the same dimensions and design as the first Temple, it lacked the splendor of its predecessor. Herod wanted to make the Temple the most magnificent of temples in the area or perhaps in the world. He lavished on this structure vast treasure. His motives were the satisfaction of his passion for beautiful and enduring buildings and the winning of his subjects' gratitude if not their love. To his sorrow, he did not win the gratitude, let alone the love, of the Jewish people. And his Temple endured for less than a century.

Herod built his Temple on a grand scale. To achieve his grandiose plan, he doubled the area of the Temple compound by building powerful sustaining walls around the Temple Mount. Like Solomon, he levelled the area by a landfill within the sustaining walls. On the southern side, however, he constructed many arches and erected the platform on them. The walls around the Temple compound were of gigantic size. Those parts of the walls which were not destroyed by subsequent conquerors are still intact and admired by everyone who sees them. The Western Wall of the Temple Mount, frequently called the Wailing Wall, is an example of the Herodian structures. The massive stones are bevelled in a distinctive style and are perfectly fitted to each other so that mortar was never used. These Herodian stones are easily identified. They can also be seen in the Tower of David near the Jaffa Gate and in Wilson's Arch, which connected the Temple Mount with the Upper City. The pillars of the arches beneath the Al-Aqsa Mosque are, to this day, admired and mistakenly called Solomon's Stables. According to the investigations of the famous archeologist, Charles Warren, the Temple area, as enlarged by Herod, is almost one and a half times greater than the area of Saint Peter's in Rome. Its splendor, too, was the pride of the nation. According to the Rabbis, "He who has not seen the Temple (of Herod) has never seen a beautiful building" (Sukkah 51b: B.B.4a).

The structure itself followed the plan of its predecessors. The ground dimensions and design were the same as those of Solomon's Temple. The height, however, was doubled, and the decorations were greatly enhanced. There was in it the Holy of Holies, which was a totally dark and empty room.[2] Adjacent to this holiest chamber was the "Holy Place" in which were the altar of incense, the seven-branched candelabrum, and the table of shewbread. This chamber was divided from the Holy of Holies by a curtain of rich texture and adornment. Then came the court of the women. In the latter court, both men and women were admitted. In front of these was the Outer Court where anyone could enter. Here merchants brought their wares for sale, mainly items needed during the performance of the Temple rites, such as animals and doves for the offerings. There were also money changers on hand to convert the pilgrims' foreign money into local currency. In this court, there was a notice in Greek and Latin warning gentiles not to come nearer to the sanctuary. The inscription reads:

> No foreigner is to enter within the balustrade and embankment around the sanctuary. Whoever is caught will have himself to blame for his death which will follow.[3]

The Temple Mount also contained a number of porches or cloisters which extended around the inside of the wall. These porches were composed of rows of lofty Corinthian pillars; thirty-seven and a half feet in height, they were covered with richly ornamented roofs. There were, all told, 162 such columns. These cloisters afforded shade in summer and shelter from the rains in winter. They also housed

---

2. In Solomon's Temple, the Ark of the Covenant with the Tablets of the Ten Commandments were housed in the Holy of Holies. These sacred items were lost during the destruction of the First Temple.

3. This inscription was not offensive to the pagans because it was common practice, in the *sancta* of ancient religions, to bar certain people from entering lest they profane the sanctity of the holy place by their impurity. In 1871, M. Clermont-Ganneau discovered the original inscription on a stone set in a wall of a small Moslem cemetery. This precious item is now in the Istanbul Museum.

the assemblies for study and the sessions of the Sanhedrin, the supreme legislative and judicial body of the nation.

In building the Temple, Herod was scrupulously careful not to violate the religious sensitivities of the people. In order not to defile the sanctity of the existing Temple, the builders within were recruited exclusively from among the priests, and in order not to interrupt the Temple ritual, the new structure was erected over the old one. Only when the new Temple was completed was the old building dismantled and removed from within.

Today, only the great platform on which Herod's Temple stood has survived. On the site of the Temple or near it, now stands the Moslem Dome of the Rock or, as it is often mistakenly called, the Mosque of Omar and, to the south of it, the Al-Aqsa Mosque. Under the Al-Aqsa Mosque, the so-called Stables of Solomon can still be seen.

Some people have tried to compare Herod with Solomon, and the resemblance is at first glance quite striking. Both Herod and Solomon were famous for their energetic building of monuments whose splendid architecture brought them fame. Both managed to maintain peace with their neighbors. Both were influenced in their architecture and style of life by foreign cultures—Solomon by Egypt and Tyre, Herod by Greece and Rome. Both Solomon and Herod fortified the city and built magnificent Temples on Mount Moriah. But this resemblance is highly misleading. While Solomon has come down in the tradition as a wise and just ruler, and even as a man of spiritual stature, the author of works that were included in the Holy Scriptures, Herod has been remembered as a cruel and bloodthirsty despot, who spared not his own kin when his suspicions were aroused. Herod was afflicted with mental aberrations and obsessed with constant fear of treacherous plots against his life and his throne. Tradition has also pictured him as a man lacking in both wisdom and piety. These contrasting personalities can hardly be regarded as similar.

Herod's great architectural enterprise on the Temple Mount gave him the fame he craved, but not the people's affection, for which he yearned even more ardently. The Temple was indeed a structure worthy of the Holy City and of the worship of the God of Israel. The Temple stood on the summit of Mount Moriah resplendent in its marvelous beauty, facing the rising sun and the Mount of Olives. Unlike the first Temple to which Solomon's name was attached, Herod's name was never associated by the Jews with his celebrated achievement. The Rabbis never mention Herod's name in connection with the Temple. He remained a despised despot who was imposed on the people by hated Rome. The Rabbis pour lavish praise on his marvelous construction, but have not a word to say about the man whose genius and dedication made the structure possible. We find in the Bible a vivid and moving description of the dedication of the first Temple. Solomon's beautiful dedication prayer is quoted in full (I Kings 8). The Bible also records in detail the dedication of the second Temple (Ezra 3). Similarly, there is a description in the Apocrypha of the rededication of the Temple after the Hasmonean victory. The Feast of Hanukkah is still observed by the Jews in commemoration of that event. However, the dedication of Herod's Temple is nowhere recorded in rabbinic literature. Herod's far-famed structure is treated as a mere continuation of the second Temple.

In this majestic sanctuary of Herod, the Jews worshipped God and atoned for their transgressions. To this Temple, the Jewish pilgrims came during the festivals, bringing their offerings and chanting the Psalms of Ascent, fifteen of which have been preserved in the Book of Psalms (Ps. 120–134). And Christians, too, revere the memory of the Temple because Jesus visited it as a worshipper, and in its precincts he did much of his teaching (John 10:22–39).

5

The War with Rome and the Fall of Jerusalem

After Herod's death in the year 4 B.C.E., his heirs could not peacefully divide the kingdom between them. Rome stepped in and took over the government of the major part of Herod's kingdom, including Jerusalem. From the year 6 C.E., Jerusalem was ruled as a Roman colony by appointed procurators. Only in the years 40 to 44 C.E. did a Jewish king, Herod Agrippa, rule in Jerusalem. He was a grandson of Herod the Great, and also a descendant of the Hasmonean family through his grandmother Queen Mariamne, Herod's wife.

Although Herod Agrippa's reign lasted only four years, he gained popularity among the Jews by saving the Temple from defilement. The "insane" Emperor Caligula had declared himself god and demanded that his subjects worship him. He ordered that a likeness of himself be installed in the Jerusalem Temple and that the Jews pay him divine honors. King Agrippa, a favorite of the Emperor, used his influence to delay the desecration. Meanwhile, the Emperor was assassinated. But Agrippa is remembered primarily for the building activities which he initiated in Jerusalem. The most important of these was the construction of a third wall on the north side of the city. He also built a new wall on the south side of the city. This wall embraced the southern section of Mount Zion.

The third wall that Agrippa began to erect included within the city the new suburb that had grown up outside the north wall. The other walls on the north side had been built by the Hasmoneans and by Herod, respectively. The Romans did not permit the completion of the third wall, because they saw in the strengthening of the city's fortification a temptation, if not an actual plan, for rebellion. The unfinished third wall was completed more than a quarter of a century later when the Jewish revolt against Rome erupted. Although the wall was completed in haste, it took much effort for the Romans to breach it.

When Agrippa died, the Romans formally annexed the land. The Roman procurators ruled despotically with the aid of Roman military contingents. They taxed the inhabitants excessively and correspondingly enriched themselves. More provoking was the procurators' ignorance of the people's religious scruples and of their spiritual commitments. They held the Jews in contempt and regarded the Jews' strange religious usages and observances as mere barbarian customs. These provocations and harassments largely account for the final outbreak of the great revolt in 66 C.E.

The revolt took the Romans by surprise and the rebels inflicted several telling defeats on the Romans. They even expelled the Roman legions from Jerusalem. The Romans soon realized that they had more than a local insurrection on their hands. It was a war of serious dimensions. They sent Vespasian, their ablest military leader, to deal with this war, and a bitter war it proved to be. Vespasian proceeded from the north, systematically subduing one stronghold after another. After conquering the Galilee and the countryside around Jerusalem, he laid siege to the city itself. During the siege, Vespasian received the news that he had been chosen Emperor. He appointed his son, Titus, to direct the difficult siege of Jerusalem, and he left for Rome. "No martial episode," says Israel Abrahams, "has ever been described with more graphic power and pathetic particularity."[1] Josephus, the historian of this war, had been the Jewish military leader entrusted with the defense of the Galilee. When the Galilee fell, Josephus surrendered to the Romans and remained in the Roman camp throughout the war. He is remembered and honored for his record, which described the battles in great detail. Some have denounced Josephus as a collaborator with the enemy. Others have defended him as a person who saw the hopelessness of the situation and tried to win better conditions for his defeated nation. Be that as it may, Josephus was a great historian and he left us a remarkable record of the war, in which he vividly and accurately described the heroic defense of Jerusalem.

But this war was hopeless. How could the courage and heroism of a small people stand up to the mighty power of Rome? From his headquarters on Mount Scopus, Titus had a glorious view of the city. Directly in front of him, within the eastern wall, stood the Temple which Herod had rebuilt. Beyond the Temple, he could clearly see the Upper City, and beyond, stood the three powerful towers that Herod had erected. To the right, he saw the three walls that protected the city on its northern side. It was on that side that the Roman legions would launch their assault. The Roman siege operations were met with great courage and death-defying heroism. Josephus describes these heroic

---

1. Israel Abrahams, *Campaigns in Palestine from Alexander the Great* (London: Oxford University Press, 1927), 35, by permission of Oxford University Press.

deeds graphically and faithfully. One can only admire the
desperate resistance of the defenders, although the hopelessness of the long drawn-out war is evident from the
start, especially if one takes into account the famine and
the divisions among the defenders. At least three military
leaders fought against each other within the beleaguered
city. They united their forces only when the enemy began
to seriously threaten the city.

After four years of bitter warfare, the Romans captured
the Temple Mount and set the Temple on fire. The defenders withdrew to the Upper City and held out for awhile.
Their doom, however, was sealed. When the Romans
finally captured the whole of Jerusalem, the city was a
shambles. The walls were demolished. Only the three
massive Herodian towers near what is now the Jaffa Gate
were left intact. According to Josephus, Titus did not
destroy these powerful fortresses so that people might see
them and appreciate the magnitude of his victory. According to Josephus 1,100,000 people perished in Jerusalem.[2]
About 100,000 were sold into slavery. Half of those who
perished were nonresidents of Jerusalem who crowded
into the beleaguered city. They had come to celebrate the
Passover and were trapped by the war. Others sought
safety within the walls or came to help defend the city.

The fall of Jerusalem and the burning of the Temple in
the year 70 c.e. were the most awesome events in the
annals of the Jewish people. Only the Nazi Holocaust has
surpassed the horrors of the war with Rome. This disaster
became a turning point in the history of the Jewish people.

The fall of Jerusalem and the burning of the Temple
became the focus of the collective memory and of the
unwavering hope of the Jewish people for two millennia.
Thenceforth, all joy was tinged with sorrow, and sorrow

2. Flavius Josephus, *The Jewish War*, Book VI, Chap. 9, No. 3.

was mingled with a dauntless faith in ultimate redemption. The shining vision of Israel's ultimate vindication became a certainty. Jerusalem was in ashes but the survivors had no doubt that in the end of days "the mountain of the Lord's house shall be established as the top of the mountains" (Isa. 2:2). Now the Jewish people were truly as the dust of the earth, but when the Messiah will come, they will be exalted above all the nations.

After the fall of Jerusalem and the destruction of the Temple, the Rabbis deliberately set themselves the task of perpetuating the memory of Jerusalem and the Temple. They not only recorded these events, but they embodied these events and rituals in living institutions and religious practices. Every Temple ritual and custom which could be disassociated from the Temple was transferred to the synagogue to be preserved for the day when the holy Temple would be rebuilt and the divine ritual reinstated. The priests (*Kohanim*) and their descendants were given the task of blessing the congregation during certain services, just as they had done in the Temple. They were also to retain their state of ritual purity by not coming near a corpse or entering a cemetery. And whenever the Torah scroll was read in the synagogue, the *Kohanim* were the first to be called to the reading. These and many other rabbinic rules have been faithfully followed to this day. Every Jew passed on to his sons their place in the hierarchy of the Temple ritual. Every boy born into a family of *Kohanim*, on reaching the age of thirteen, joined his father in the performance of his priestly duties in the synagogue.

The Rabbinic decrees were not limited to those of priestly birth. Every Jew was to keep the psalmist's oath:

If I forget thee, O Jerusalem,
Let my right hand forget her cunning . . . .
If I set not Jerusalem
Above my chiefest joy (Ps. 137:5–6).

When a Jewish couple was married, the ceremony was concluded with the bridegroom breaking a glass as a memorial of the destruction of Jerusalem and the holy Temple. And when the married couple moved into their home, they left a spot on the wall unpainted as a reminder of Jerusalem's desolation.

By far more effective has been the incorporation, in the cycle of the synagogue and private worship, of many prayers for Jerusalem's redemption and the Temple's restoration. The observant Jew prays for the restoration of Jerusalem daily—morning, noon, and night.

> And let our eyes behold Thy return in mercy to Zion. Praised art Thou, O Lord, Who restorest Thy divine presence unto Zion.

After each meal, the Jew recites among the benedictions of the grace:

> Have mercy, O Lord our God, upon Israel Thy people, upon Jerusalem Thy city, upon Zion, the abiding place of Thy glory . . . . And rebuild Jerusalem the holy city speedily in our days. Praised art Thou, O Lord, who in Thy compassion rebuildest Jerusalem.

Jerusalem's desolation was especially bewailed on the anniversary of the catastrophe, on the Ninth of Av. As it happened, the anniversaries of the destruction of the first Temple and of the second Temple coincided. Hence, the mourning was intensified. The Ninth of Av was a day of fasting and lamentations. It was a national fast that ranked second only to that of the Day of Atonement. Indeed, the Jews regarded themselves as permanent "mourners of Zion and Jerusalem" so that, in offering condolences to a mourner, the standard formula has been, "May God comfort you among the rest of the mourners of Zion and

Jerusalem." So great was the shock of the disaster that all music was prohibited, even in the synagogue. In time, this stringent rule was relaxed and applied only to instrumental music.

The endurance of the Jewish national memory and the depth of the nation's faith were the two main ingredients that made for survival after the national disaster. The faith in God's justice and mercy strengthened the messianic ideal. The redemption of Israel was inevitable, for divine justice demanded the vindication of Jewish suffering and humiliation. It was a comforting idea, but it was also a root cause of another national disaster, the second war against Rome.

6

The Second War with Rome

When Titus returned to Rome, he left the Tenth Legion in Jerusalem to keep order and prevent new uprisings from breaking out. The Roman soldiers were stationed in the western part of the city where the Citadel is now located. Gradually, the city began to rise from its ruins. In time, the war restraints were relaxed and Jews were permitted to return. But the wounds of the war were not quickly healed. The destruction of the Temple was a festering wound, and the frightful destitution that afflicted all ranks of the population were blamed on the hated enemy. The Romans were insensitive to the plight of the defeated rebels. The taxes they levied were, according to rabbinic records, unconscionable. The survivors of the war were resentful of the hateful enemy who ruled with a spirit of vengeance. And the new generation that grew up after the war was raised in an atmosphere of hate for "Rome the Wicked."

In this atmosphere of despair, only a messiah could bring redemption. The expectation of divine help by means of "an anointed of God" was widespread. How could God "hide His face" from the evil, oppression, and brutality that prevailed in the land and especially in the Holy City? A redeemer, they felt, was bound to appear. And whenever the Jewish people ardently yearned for the Messiah, a messiah usually appeared. This time, he appeared in the person of a brave and skillful warrior who inspired the people with faith in his ability to bring redemption from the hated foe.

Suffering alone would not have roused the people to a second war with Rome. The memory of the disaster of the last revolt was too fresh to indulge in wild illusions of victory. But active persecution was added to oppression, and the burden became unbearable. Hadrian, the Roman emperor, chose to enact what seemed to him a minor item of legislation. He prohibited the circumcision of Jewish children. Little did he suspect that he had struck something vital in Judaism—the Covenant of Abraham, no less. The cup of suffering was running over. This was the proverbial last straw. The Messiah was now expected momentarily. If the people were not worthy of redemption, the Roman attempt to abrogate the Covenant of Abraham would surely move God to humble the proud oppressor.

The "messiah" who appeared was a military leader by the name of Bar Kozeva, the Son of Kozeva, indicating his paternity. When the revolt failed, some saw in his name a hint of his having been a false messiah, for the word Kozeva also means a lie. Bar Kozeva, they said, indicated that he was the "Son of a Lie." But this was hindsight. At the time of the uprising, he was received with universal enthusiasm. He was called Bar Kokhba, Son of a Star, a hint of his divine mission. Bar Kokhba's early life is totally unknown. He appears only during the revolt, when he proved himself a man of military stature. He was strong, courageous, and firm in the conduct of the revolt. Many legends grew up around his physical prowess, his fearless-

ness, and his determined leadership. He aroused enthusiasm and confidence not only among the common folk but
also among some of the most respected religious and
learned leaders. The greatest scholar of the day, Rabbi
Akiba, and his many disciples were among his dedicated
followers.

In the year 132 c.e., only two generations after the great
disaster of the year 70, the revolt broke out with surprising
fury. The Roman legion stationed in Jerusalem was defeated and an independent Jewish state was launched.
Coins were struck with the inscription "For the Freedom of
Jerusalem." More important, an altar was hastily erected
on the Temple Mount and the Temple ritual was reinstated.
But the war had only begun. The Romans, realizing the
gravity of the situation, brought their most celebrated
general, Julius Severus, from far-off Britain to assume
command of the Roman legions in Palestine. Severus
gathered a formidable army, and soon the most ferocious
battles the land had ever known were being fought by the
mighty Roman army and the death-defying Jewish rebels.
After initial Jewish victories, the struggle settled down to a
war of attrition. The self-sacrificing courage and the fa-
natical desperation of the rebels prolonged the war and
multiplied the casualties on both sides. Tradition has it
that rivers of blood streamed in the streets of Jerusalem;
the casualties were over half a million dead. The Roman
casualties were so great that the emperor, in reporting to
the Roman Senate, omitted the usual phrase, "I and the
army are well." After three years of bloody battles, Roman
power prevailed. The last battle was fought at Betar. Betar,
too, fell on the Ninth of Av, and it was added to the
disasters that had befallen the Jewish people on that
anniversary. The fast and mourning on that anniversary
thereafter commemorated the destruction of the first Temple
in 586 b.c.e., the destruction of the second Temple in 70,

and the failure of the courageous but foolhardy attempt to topple the superpower of Rome in 135.

The lament for Jerusalem's fate in 586 B.C.E. was as applicable to the new disaster as it had been to the one of 70. For almost two thousand years thereafter, the Jews fasted and wept for the new disaster along with the former ones:

> How doth the city sit solitary,
>   That was full of people!
> How is she become as a widow!
>   She that was great among the nations,
> And princess among the provinces,
>   How is she become tributary! (Lam. 1:1).

7

Jerusalem, a Pagan City

The Roman victory was far from glorious. This may be the reason for Hadrian's decision to liquidate Judaism and to obliterate Jerusalem from the map. He forbade the study and the teaching of the holy writings, the observance of the Sabbath and the religious festivals, and the initiation of children into the covenant of Abraham. The Hadrianic persecutions are vividly recorded in the liturgy, especially in the dirges bewailing the martyrs who died "for the sanctification of God's name."

The City of Jerusalem was totally demolished and a plow was run over the site to symbolize that the city was eternally erased from the map. On the site of Jerusalem, a new pagan city was built in honor of the Roman gods, the Capitoline triad of Jupiter, Juno, and Minerva. The new city also honored the emperor, whose family name was Aelius. The new Roman city was therefore named *Aelia Capitolina*. The city was laid out as a typical Roman city, with two intersecting wide streets ending in the main gates

41

to the city. The street which ran from north to south was known as the *Cardo*, and the street which ran from east to west was known as the *Decumannus*. These main streets divided the city into four quarters, which roughly correspond today to the Moslem, Christian, Jewish, and Armenian Quarters of the Old City. The Cardo ran from the Damascus gate in the north to a gate in the south wall. The latter gate was then located somewhat to the east of the present Zion Gate.[1] The Decumannus ran from what is now the Jaffa Gate down David Street, up the Street of the Chain to the Temple Mount. The street then skirted the Temple Mount and ended with the Lions' or St. Stephen's Gate. Inside the Damascus Gate, there was an open place with a lofty column in the center.

Near the intersection of the main streets was the Forum, which was a distinguishing adjunct of every Roman city. Today, the Muristan Bazaar, near the Church of the Holy Sepulchre, is on the site of that Forum. Hadrian provided his city with other typical Roman institutions such as a theater, public baths, and triumphal arches. One of these arches is the traditional Ecce Homo Arch in the Via Dolorosa. On the site of the Jewish Temple, Hadrian erected a pagan temple in honor of Jupiter, with an equestrian statue of himself in front of it. On the site of the Holy Sepulchre, he built a temple in honor of Aphrodite. Jews and Christians were forbidden to enter the city on pain of death.

The walls of the city were rebuilt. They were shorter than those of Herod's days. Their new contours have been retained to the present day. The southern wall excluded the ancient City of David and most of Mount Zion, as it still does today. On the northern side, one can still see an

---

1. The Zion Gate was moved westward when the city walls were rebuilt by the Turks in the sixteenth century.

arched entry below the bridge at the entrance to the Damascus Gate. This gate is a relic of the Roman wall on the north side of the city. The east and west walls followed the foundations of the former walls.

The Roman city *Aelia Capitolina* is clearly visible on a mosaic map that was discovered in 1897 in the ruins of a church at Madeba, east of the Dead Sea. This map dates from about 550. On it one can see a main columned street which ran from north to south, that is, from the present Damascus Gate to a gate in the southern wall somewhat east of the present Zion Gate. In front of the northern (Damascus) gate, one can see an open place with a column in its center. On this map one can see that *Aelia Capitolina* differed somewhat from the typical pattern of a Roman city in a couple of details. The first of these is that there were two parallel main streets running from north to south, as is still the case today. The two streets still start out from the open space near the Damascus Gate. The street running from west to east could not run straight but had to skirt the Temple Mount. In all other aspects, *Aelia Capitolina* was a typical Roman city.

The Romans surely thought that they had solved "the Jewish problem." They had liquidated Judaism and permanently erased Jerusalem from the map. But the Jews made the city of Tiberius their temporary spiritual center, and they kept alive the memory of Jerusalem. Even the Palestinian Talmud that was compiled in Tiberius, they called the Jerusalem Talmud, by which name it is known to this day.

The distinguished scholar, Israel Abrahams, writing during the British occupation of Jerusalem in the days of the Mandate, sums up this sad era in Jerusalem's history in these striking words:

Hadrian drew the plough over the Temple Hill, founded his brand new Aelia Capitolina, and wrote *finis* over the ruins of Jerusalem. But destiny laughs at shortsighted finalities, and while Aelia Capitolina as a name for Jerusalem is known only to antiquarians, Jerusalem is the name which it continued to bear. So far from remaining a pagan city, Jerusalem the Holy, or *el-Kuds*, was destined to be a meeting place of the daughter faiths born of Judaism—too often the battleplace of children fighting over their mother's grave.[2]

Like Jerusalem, the Jewish people was once declared extinct. It was more than 3,000 years ago that Israel's total annihilation was proudly declared by Pharaoh Merneptha. On a stela raised to commemorate his victories, he had inscribed: "Israel is destroyed. The seed of Jacob is no more." This stela is presently on exhibit in the Cairo Museum. This, in fact, is Israel's introduction on the stage of history. Pharaoh Merneptha was the forerunner of other rulers of vast empires, Hadrian among them, who declared: "Come and let us cut them off from being a nation; that the name of Israel may be no more in remembrance" (Ps. 83:5). Jerusalem has shared Israel's fate and, like Israel, has shared eternal life, notwithstanding the evil counsel of mighty tyrants.

The new city, *Aelia Capitolina*, existed as a pagan city for almost two centuries, from the suppression of the Bar Kokhba revolt in the second century to the fourth century, when Constantine issued his edict of religious toleration. Physically, the new city existed for about 500 years, until it was captured and devastated by the Persians in 614.

Despite the ambitious Roman building activity, Jerusalem remained a small provincial town. Throughout the two centuries of its pagan existence, *Aelia Capitolina* was of

---

2. Israel Abrahams, *Campaigns in Palestine from Alexander the Great* (London: Oxford University Press, 1927), 40, by permission of Oxford University Press.

little consequence and is hardly heard of. Only the Jews continued to mourn Jerusalem's destruction and to pray for its restoration. Also, some Christian pilgrims managed to visit the city.

As already mentioned, one of Hadrian's ordinances prohibited the Jews to enter or even come within sight of the new city. However, the city did not remain *Judenrein* for too long. The Bordeaux Pilgrim who visited the city in 333 speaks of Jews coming annually to lament the destruction of the Temple.

The name "Aelia," without its pagan "Capitolina," continued to be used by many Christians even after Constantine restored the name of Jerusalem to the city. Even as late as the seventh century, the name Aelia was still used by some Christians. After that, the pagan name was forgotten and Jerusalem was again the universal name of the Holy City.

8

The Holy City of Christendom

Constantine I became Emperor of Rome in 313. It took another decade for him to defeat his opponents, consolidate his power, and become the sole ruler of the Roman Empire. With Constantine's rise to power, the Byzantine period in Jerusalem's history began, and it lasted fully three centuries, until the invasion of the Moslems in 638.

Constantine's conversion to Christianity may have taken place as early as 312. According to some, his conversion was partially motivated by political considerations, as is indicated by his retention of the post of head or Pontifex Maximus of the Roman Pantheon all his life. Also significant is the nature of the dedication of his new capital. When Constantinople was dedicated in 330, the ceremonies were half Christian and half pagan. Finally, Constantine's actual baptism took place only shortly before his death in 337. However, throughout his reign, he encouraged Christianity and gradually repressed paganism. He is credited with pro-Christian legislation such as prohibiting

Jews to convert their slaves to Judaism. More significant is Constantine's convening the Council of Nicaea in 325, hoping thereby to heal the rift in the ranks of Christianity caused by the views of Arius about the nature of Jesus. But the most telling act testifying to his dedication to Christianity was his enduring monument in Jerusalem—the Church of the Holy Sepulchre, which has had a massive impact on the city's character as a holy city in Christendom.

Actually, Jerusalem's role in Christianity began long before the days of Constantine. According to the Acts of the Apostles, the first Christian congregation gathered in the room of the Last Supper on Mount Zion shortly after the death of Jesus. This group, under the spiritual leadership of James the Less, was called the Mother of Churches. The first Christians were of Jewish extraction, and the problem soon arose whether converts to Christianity could be recruited among the gentiles. At a council held in Jerusalem in the year 50, it was decided that gentiles could be admitted to the new faith. During the Roman siege of Jerusalem in the year 70, the members of the small Christian community left for Pella in Transjordan. This was regarded by the Jews as an act of desertion. After the total destruction of Jerusalem in 137, the Christians were also persecuted by the Romans and their holy places were, according to Christian tradition, obliterated. When Constantine became emperor, he asked the Bishop of Jerusalem to discover the site of Golgotha where Jesus was crucified and of the Holy Sepulchre where Jesus was buried. There had been a persistent tradition that the pagan Temple of Venus was erected on the site of the Holy Sepulchre. The Bishop validated the tradition. Constantine therefore had the Temple of Venus demolished and ordered the erection of a fitting church whose glory would surpass all monumental structures.

The church consisted of two structures separated by a

court. The first was a circular building around the Holy Sepulchre. The floor of the church was levelled, leaving in the center the rock in which was the cavern of the Holy Sepulchre. This holy place was enclosed by a small chapel, the exterior of which was encased in marble slabs, and its conical roof was covered with tiles, some of which were overlaid with silver and some with gold. The circular building around the Sepulchre was topped with a cupola that was open in the center to admit daylight. This building was known as the Anastasis (the Resurrection).

East of this building was a court with colonnades in which was a rock called Golgotha. A monumental cross marking the spot of the crucifixion was enclosed in a structure. At the base of this rock, there was a cave which was called the "Chapel of Adam." The fissure in the Rock, it was claimed, was formed by the earthquake recorded in Matthew's account of the Crucifixion (Mat. 27:51–54). In later centuries, the "center of the world" was also located in this court.

Beyond this court was Constantine's Basilica, called the Martyrion. This structure, which was the main church, was a magnificent building, the pride and glory of the Christians. Beyond the Basilica, there was another court with colonnades, which opened to the market street.

Jerusalem's role as the Holy City of Christianity was further enhanced by the emperor's mother, Queen Helena. She was a pious woman with an inordinate zeal for the propagation of her new faith. In 325, Queen Helena came to Jerusalem on a pilgrimage and embarked on a search for Christian relics. She was, beyond doubt, the luckiest of archeologists for she found in her excavations everything she sought. Her main concern was to find the True Cross. The excavations she initiated yielded not only the True Cross but also the two crosses of the thieves. She had difficulty in deciding which of the crosses was the true one. Fortunately, a miracle came to her aid. The crosses were brought to the bedside of a sick woman. The thieves' crosses had no effect on the sick woman. But when the True Cross was brought in, the patient was immediately cured. Helena also found the nails with which Jesus was fastened to the cross and the crown of thorns that Jesus wore at the crucifixion. She even found the original board with the inscription, "Jesus of Nazareth, King of the Jews." The crypt in which the crosses were found was cleared and it became a Christian shrine of prime importance. Queen Helena also built memorials to some of the other sacred events associated with Jesus' ministry, crucifixion, and resurrection. These memorials have been hallowed in Christendom. To be sure, there are some who question the authenticity of Helena's discoveries. However, her finds have become part of the heritage of most Christians, both Oriental and Occidental.

After Constantine and his mother Helena erected their memorials, Jerusalem became a magnet for Christian pilgrims. Priests, monks, nuns, and pious hermits were drawn to the holy places. Especially during the Easter season, the pilgrims came in large numbers, and the city was alive with people and religious devotions in the churches.

Two other emperors merit consideration because of their impact on Jerusalem's fate. These emperors are Julian the Apostate and Theodosius the Great. In the year 361, Constantine's nephew, Flavius Claudius Julianus, became emperor. Although he had been brought up as a Christian, he saw in Christianity an alien culture that was displacing the authentic civilization of the Romans. He became zealous for the cause of reinstating the old Roman pantheon. His anti-Christian policy earned him the title "Julian the Apostate," by which he is known in history. But to Judaism, he showed every consideration. He even indicated an interest in the rebuilding of the Temple on Mount Moriah. In a letter addressed to the "Community of the Jews," sent at the beginning of 363, he spoke of the abolition of the heavy taxes that had been imposed upon the Jews, and concluded his letter with these words:

> Thus should you do in order that when I return safely from the Persian war, I may restore the Holy City of Jerusalem, and rebuild it at my own expense, even as you have for so many years desired it to be restored; and therein will I unite with you in giving praise to the Almighty.[1]

Jewish hopes were raised to a high pitch. Some Jews saw in Julian's promise "the finger of God"; the Messiah was surely not far away. Julian's plans, however, were not implemented because he did not return from the Persian war. Before the year was out, Julian had died, and nothing came of his promise. His whole reign lasted only two years (361–363). Tradition has it that the building of the Temple was actually begun. But no sooner did the workers reach the foundations, than flames burst out and the workmen fled. The work was suspended, never to be resumed. This fire, says Christian tradition, was a sign of divine wrath. Jewish tradition says that the fire was a sign that the time set for Israel's redemption had not yet arrived. Some rationalists have attempted a scientific explanation, that the mysterious flames were caused by noxious gas in the subterranean chambers catching fire. The most rational explanation seems to be that the work stopped because the prime mover of the enterprise had died and his plan died with him.

The success of Christianity reached its peak when Theodosius the Great became Emperor in 379. He completed what Constantine had begun. Theodosius made Christianity the official religion of the empire: he tore down the heathen sanctuaries in the Holy Land, and encouraged

---

1. Michael Adler, "The Emperor Julian and the Jews," *The Jewish Quarterly Review* Vol. 5 (1914–1915): 624.

benefactors to subsidize the construction of churches and convents. Among these memorial structures were the Sepulchre of the Virgin Mary in the Kidron Valley, and the Church of St. Peter in Gallicantu on Mount Zion.

Jerusalem grew and expanded. A vast building activity began, and many churches, convents, and hospices were erected by pious benefactors. In the sixth-century Madeba map, mentioned above, the Church of the Holy Sepulchre is featured prominently, and the city is shown to be full of churches, monasteries, and hospices. Among the more recently identified archeological remains of that period are those of the vast New Church of St. Mary called the "Nea," which was erected by the Emperor Theodosius who ruled from 518 to 565. In the middle of the fifth century, the Empress Eudocia extended the city's wall on the south to include Mount Zion. This, too, is indicated on the Madeba map. Also unearthed recently was the central broad street, known as the Cardo, that ran from the Damascus Gate to the southern wall.

Some of the pilgrims who came to Jerusalem recorded their experiences. These writings have provided the modern student with much valuable data. The first pilgrim to leave us a record of his visit in Jerusalem was a nameless pilgrim from Bordeaux who visited Jerusalem in 333. His itinerary, despite its brevity, is of value to scholars, because it contains comments on Jerusalem's topography, a subject that has baffled many a scholar.

The Byzantine period also witnessed a slight relaxation of Hadrian's ban on the entry of Jews into Jerusalem. Jews were now permitted, once a year, on the anniversary of the destruction of the Temple (Tishah B'Av—the Ninth of Av), to assemble at a distance from the Temple Mount and to mourn the loss of their holy shrine. The place of this annual assembly of lamentation seems to have been on the Mount of Olives, which was outside the city but within sight of the Temple Mount. In strange contrast, the Christians held the Temple Mount in contempt and used it as a dumping place for their garbage. This practice seems to have been instituted as a means of demonstrating the degradation of Judaism.

In 394, the Roman Empire was partitioned. The Holy Land naturally became part of the Eastern Empire. Life in Jerusalem remained uneventful during the Byzantine period except for a disastrous invasion early in the seventh century when Chosroes, King of Persia, invaded Asia Minor. His aim was to avenge the murder of his father-in-law. In 614, Chosroes overran the Holy Land and, after a siege of only twenty days, captured Jerusalem. The churches were plundered and then demolished by fire. The Church of the Holy Sepulchre, too, was burned down completely. Among the captives taken to Persia was the Patriarch of Jerusalem, and in the plunder taken as booty were many holy relics, the most precious of which was the wooden cross that Helena had recovered. This relic had been preserved in a silver casket in Constantine's Basilica.

After the capitulation, some of the inhabitants rebelled and killed the Persian governor. The invaders retaliated with savage vengeance. They sacked and pillaged the whole city. This was the end of Hadrian's Roman city, for very little of it remained after the Persians finished their brief occupation of the city.

The Persians stayed in Jerusalem only fourteen years. Emperor Heraclius fought them successfully and reconquered the lost territories. In 639, he entered Jerusalem barefoot, bearing the holy relic of the cross. He restored the Church of the Holy Sepulchre, but the church was now much inferior in splendor to the original structure that Constantine had built.

The Persian war weakened both Byzantium and Persia so that when, less than a decade later, a new invader entered the arena, the two empires were too weak to resist. They both fell easily to this new power.

9

A Holy City of Islam

Emperor Heraclius' victory over the Persians was of little avail. Within a decade, he was defeated by a new wave of conquerors, the Saracens, whose stay in Jerusalem lasted considerably longer than the brief sojourn of the Persians.

The new conquerors came from the Arabian desert where a new religion had been born. In a short time, this religious movement became a world power. The founder of the new religion was a man named Muhammad (570–632), a man of humble birth, little education, and a lowly occupation. He was only a camel driver and practically illiterate. Islam, as the new religion was called, was based on the central tenet that God is One. The new faith was encumbered neither by the complicated religious laws of Judaism, nor by such disputable dogmas of Christianity as the Trinity, the Incarnation, and the Sacraments. The new religion spread with phenomenal speed. Only a century after the Prophet's death, Islam had won over millions of adherents in such far-flung regions as Syria, Mesopotamia,

Persia and central Asia, Egypt, North Africa, and Spain. The Holy Land, too, was swept into the fold of the new religion. When Jerusalem fell to the invaders, a new era in its history was initiated.

The Caliph Omar, who led the army of Islam in its first *Jihad* or holy war, defeated the Byzantine Emperor Heraclius in the decisive battle of the River Yarmuk. When the Islamic armies approached Jerusalem, the city was defenseless. The Christians were called upon to capitulate or face utter decimation. The Patriarch of Jerusalem agreed to surrender, but only to the Caliph himself. Omar acceded to the Patriarch's request. The meeting between the two men must have been startling. The contrast between the resplendent vestments of the Byzantine prelate and the coarse raiment of the Caliph was surely amazing. The Patriarch must have been taken by surprise. And he must have been equally astonished by the terms of surrender. For that age of religious intolerance, Omar's terms were generous and humane, although, by modern standards, they appear harsh and humiliating. There was no blood bath. Whoever wished to leave the city was given safety in person and property until he had reached his destination. The infidels, that is Christians and Jews, were not to be constrained in the matter of their religion or molested. The infidels could worship in their respective churches or synagogues, but they were not to build new places of worship without special permission. Pilgrimages were not interrupted, but all infidels were to pay an annual poll tax and were to treat Moslems with the greatest respect. They were also to extend to Moslems the rights of hospitality, rise to receive them, and accord them the place of honor in all assemblies. The infidels were not to carry arms or ride astride their animals, nor were Christians to wear or publicly exhibit the sign of the cross, or sound church bells, or raise their voices in lamentation for the dead.

These and similar stipulations were incorporated in the terms of surrender.

The Moslems did not come merely to settle accounts or to wreak vengeance on a hated prince or people. They came to stay. Therefore, they took over the holiest place of Judaism, the Temple Mount, and turned it into a Moslem holy place of high rank. This was the beginning of the process of making Jerusalem a holy city of Islam.

After the surrender of Jerusalem in 638 had been arranged, Omar turned his attention to his religious concerns. Jerusalem, though far removed from the centers of Islam in the Arabian desert, already occupied a place of honor in the Moslem tradition. Muhammad knew about Jerusalem from his contact with Jews and Christians. Just as he borrowed freely many of his theological ideas from Judaism and Christianity, so he also borrowed the concept of Jerusalem's sanctity, which derived from having harbored Solomon's Temple. More important for Moslems was the tradition that Jerusalem was the city to which Muhammad had made his famous nocturnal journey on his miraculous steed, Buraq; and from Jerusalem, he ascended to heaven. The spot from which he was said to have ascended was the place where once stood Solomon's Temple.

Omar's first concern was to identify the holy site of Solomon's Temple. He asked the Patriarch to show him that holy place. The Patriarch was reluctant because the Christians had been dumping dung and garbage on the Temple Mount as a means of harassing and irritating the Jews. When the Patriarch finally led him to the Temple Mount, Omar had the place thoroughly cleaned of the accumulated dung. Then, he built nearby a temporary wooden mosque and led the faithful in prayer. This mosque was to the south of the Rock, where the Al-Aqsa Mosque now stands. No wonder that the Temple platform became a very holy site for the Moslems. They named the compound

Haram al-Sharif (the Noble Sanctuary), and Jerusalem became *El Kuds* (the Holy City).

About fifty years later, in 691, the Caliph Abd-al-Malik (685–705) built a magnificent monument on the site where King Solomon's Temple once stood—the Dome of the Rock or, as it is often mistakenly called, the Mosque of Omar, though it is not a mosque. His heir, the Caliph al-Walid (705–715) built the Al-Aqsa Mosque on the southern part of the Temple Mount. These two far-famed Moslem shrines, along with the fountains, minarets, open pulpits, and slender arches that were built by pious Moslems, helped raise Jerusalem to high sanctity in Islam. The city is the third holiest in Islam. Only Mecca and Medina rank higher.

People have speculated on the Caliph Abd-al-Malik's motivation in the construction of that magnificent structure, the Dome of the Rock. According to some, he was motivated by political and economic rather than religious considerations. Jerusalem's importance could not have been a chief consideration. Neither Abd-al-Malik nor any of the Moslem rulers made Jerusalem the capital of their kingdom. It was not even made the capital of the province. However, Mecca and Medina had rebelled against the Caliph Abd-al-Malik. He, therefore, wanted a shrine in Jerusalem to eclipse the rebellious holy cities and to divert the Moslem pilgrims from Mecca and Medina to Jerusalem. Moslems were urged to make pilgrimages to Jerusalem, the reward of which was heaven.

Other scholars have pointed to another motivation. A mosaic inscription around the colonnade of the Dome is directed sharply against Christianity. It contains anti-Christian statements, such as:

"He (God) neither begetteth nor is begotten."
"He taketh not unto Himself a son,
and none can be a partner to His kingdom."
"Believe then in God and His prophets and

do not say that there are three gods."
"It is not for God to take unto Himself a son,
far be it from Him."

On the basis of these and similar inscriptions, some
scholars have concluded that the main purpose in con-
structing the Dome of the Rock was the Caliph's desire to
eclipse the Christian Church of the Holy Sepulchre.

While the actual motives of Abd-al-Malik remain in
doubt, his shrine is surely a glorious monument of architectural skill. He allocated to this enterprise all the rev-
enues of Egypt during the seven years, from 684 to 691,
that it took to erect the building. Its admirers, and there
are many of them, claim that it is a gem of beauty and
grace unequalled anywhere. Ever since its erection, it has
been by far the outstanding landmark of Jerusalem. The
lower part of the structure is an octagon, each side mea-
suring sixty-seven feet in length. The diameter is about 170
feet, and so is its height. The upper portion of the structure
is a gilded dome. The building is basically the same today
as it was when erected in the seventh century.

A curious forgery was perpetrated on the dedication
inscription. The name of Caliph Abd-al-Malik was erased
and in its place was inserted the name of Abdullah al-
Mamun, a caliph who lived more than a hundred years
later. The forger, however, failed to change the date in the
inscription. This oversight has made the forgery quite
transparent. But Abdullah al-Mamun deserves some ap-
probation for, in 831, he completed the building of the
Al-Aqsa Mosque which the Caliph al-Walid had begun
more than a century before.

The Al-Aqsa Mosque, too, is an impressive structure. It is
spacious enough to accommodate thousands of worshippers, and its dome is prominent enough to be a landmark
of Jerusalem. The mosque has suffered from a number of
calamities, mostly earthquakes. It was therefore rebuilt

several times and very little remains of the original structure.

As time passed, Jerusalem's sanctity became a central doctrine of Islam. Moslems are urged to make pilgrimages to Jerusalem after they have been to Mecca and Medina. A prayer recited in a Mosque of Jerusalem is equivalent to forty prayers elsewhere. If one cannot make a pilgrimage to Jerusalem, he should provide oil for the lamps of El Kuds. As long as these lamps are burning, the donor is remembered in the prayers of the angels.

Omar imposed a reign of "contemptuous toleration." This policy was already demonstrated in his terms of capitulation. The Moslem rulers who followed Omar continued these guidelines and, at times, improved on them. To their credit it should be said that the ban on Jewish residence in Jerusalem, which had been partially in force from the time of Hadrian, was now lifted. Jews were also permitted to pray near the site of the Temple. And, like the Christians, they were granted security of person and property. As infidels, they had to pay the poll tax and were forbidden to dress like Moslems, to carry arms, to ride astride an animal, or to set foot on the holy precincts of the Haram. Therefore, neither Christian nor Jew entered that compound for hundreds of years until modern times. Nor was a church bell heard in Jerusalem until the nineteenth century.

More irritating than the official discriminations were the Moslems' spiteful "pinpricks." Near the important churches and synagogues, mosques were built with tall minarets overtopping the infidel houses of worship to indicate the superiority of Islam. Next to the Church of the Holy Sepulchre stands an imposing mosque. Moslem tradition claims that Omar prayed on that spot. Hence, it is proper that a memorial mosque be erected there. And, next to the Ramban and Hurvah synagogues in the very center of the Jewish Quarter, a mosque was erected with a minaret overtopping the lofty dome of the Hurvah synagogue. More pernicious was the establishment of a tannery next to the Church of the Holy Sepulchre, so that the offensive smells might torment the Christians during their religious services. Similarly, a slaughterhouse was located next to the Yohanan ben Zakkai Synagogue. But the most painful humiliation for the Christians was the appointment of a Moslem custodian to the Church of the Holy Sepulchre. The keys to the Church were given by Sultan Ayub to two Moslem families; one kept the keys and the other opened and closed the Church's doors. No Christian service could be held unless that Moslem custodian opened the church doors, and no Christian could enter for worship without paying an entrance fee to the Moslem custodian.

Yet life was not too oppressive. Christians and Jews were permitted to manage their own religious and communal affairs. However, the fortunes of the infidels depended on the good will of the caliphs and, even more so, on the rapacious appetites of their pashas or governors. The general appearance of Jerusalem, except for the clearance of the Temple Mount and the eminent structures upon it, remained practically unchanged.

After the early glories of the Moslem conquerors, there followed a period of relative calm. Endless squabbles between rival clans and sects periodically disturbed the tranquility of these dreary centuries. But toward the end of the tenth century, evil winds began to blow from North Africa. In 969, the Holy Land was captured by the Fatimids, an Egyptian dynasty that had risen to power in North Africa and laid claim to the caliphate of Baghdad. One of the Fatimids, al-Hakim, ascended the throne in 996 and reigned for 25 years.

Al-Hakim was a veritable scourge and his reign was one of blood and terror. His subjects suffered and so did Jerusalem. The peak of his madness was an edict, in 1010, to destroy all churches and synagogues in his realm. The destruction was carried out with rigor and thoroughness. The Church of the Holy Sepulchre was completely demolished. Only the Sepulchre itself was left unharmed. These acts of destruction and bloodshed laid the foundation for the First Crusade, which was launched at the end of the century.

In the last years of his reign, al-Hakim declared himself to be God's manifestation in the flesh, and he demanded from his subjects worship and adoration. However, his reign of terror came to an end when he was assassinated in 1021. His body was never found. Hence, some came to believe that he was actually divine and awaited his reappearance in a new manifestation. He would then, said his followers, judge the earth. The Druse are apparently still expecting his return.

When the long maniacal rule of al-Hakim came to an end, life began to settle down. In 1042, the rebuilding of the Church of the Holy Sepulchre was begun. In that year, Constantine IX, surnamed Monomachus, became emperor, and he was largely responsible for the reconstruction. In 1048, the Anastasis and the Golgotha Church were completed. The Martyrion, however, was not rebuilt. It was still a heap of ruins when another calamity befell Jerusalem.

The Seljuk Turks invaded the land in 1071, captured Jerusalem, and ruled the Holy City for almost twenty years. They pillaged the city and cruelly maltreated the population. This new disaster gave the final impetus to the launching of the First Crusade. Although the Seljuk Turks looted the population, they left the city intact. From the time of the Seljuk invasion, the Arabs did not rule Jerusalem again until 1948, when the Jordanians captured the Old City and ruled it for nineteen years.

10

The Rise of the Latin Kingdom of Jerusalem

In 1095, Pope Urban II launched the First Crusade to deliver the Holy Land from the hands of the infidels and to take possession of the Holy Sepulchre in Jerusalem. Knights and peasants, men of piety, and men who sought adventure joined the ranks of the Crusade. On their standards, the Crusaders had an emblem that came to be known as the Jerusalem Cross and is part of the Franciscan Order's seal. The Cross consists of a large square cross with four small crosses in the four spaces formed by the vertical and the transverse arms of the larger cross.[1]

The motives for the Christian conquest of Jerusalem and

---

1. This cross was not invented by the Crusaders. Archeologists have found such a cross in Transjordan dating back centuries before the First Crusade. Popular explanations for the Jerusalem cross are: (1) The five crosses represent the five nations that took part in the Crusades—Italy, Spain, Germany, France, and England; (2) the five crosses represent the five wounds that were inflicted on the body of Jesus during the crucifixion.

the Holy Land are complex and manifold. No doubt many Crusaders joined out of pure piety. They were concerned for the holy places and especially for the Holy Sepulchre. It is equally certain that many joined out of selfish consider- ations, such as love of adventure, expectation of loot, or escape from the threat of imprisonment for crimes they had committed. The immediate cause, however, was the alarm aroused by conditions in the Holy Land after its conquest by the Seljuk Turks. The invaders had murdered, pillaged, and desecrated the holy places. These atrocities inflamed Christian emotions everywhere. The Seljuk con- quest of Asia Minor had also cut the overland pilgrim route and made pilgrimage to the Holy Land hazardous.

Some historians, however, see in the Crusade the work of a scheming Pope whose aim was to restore the Roman Catholic Church's prestige by a holy war; at the same time, he hoped to restore peace to Europe by diverting the energies of the warlike European nobility to the East. Still others have seen the main motivation of the Crusade in the nobility's hunger for land, gold, and power. As evidence, these people quote Pope Urban II, who said at an assem- blage of feudal lords: "If you must have blood, bathe your hands in the blood of the infidels. . . . Soldiers of hell, become soldiers of the living God!" In sum, why fight one another? Better fight the Saracens.

No doubt the motivations were many, both noble and mundane. These contrasting motivations were clearly re- flected in the behavior of the Crusaders both during and after the war. Nobility, piety, courage, and sublime self- sacrifice were mingled with cruelty, superstition, greed, treachery, and even depravity. Some of the negative ele- ments of the Crusade were revealed at the very outset, en route to the Holy Land. The Crusaders initiated their holy war with a series of massacres in the Rhineland where one Jewish community after another were slaughtered. Eight hundred were massacred at Worms, one thousand at

Mayence, and so on. The Jewish ideal of martyrdom was not born at Massadah. The mass suicide at Massadah was tragic and heroic, but martyrdom as a national ideal has its roots in the brutalities of the Crusades, when whole communities committed suicide rather than fall into the hands of the Crusaders. Those who did fall into the Crusaders' hands chose to die as martyrs rather than accept the offer of baptism. It was then that martyrdom became a widespread national ideal. Martyrs became the beloved of God and the revered "holy ones" of the people.

It has been estimated that the Crusaders had started out with over a million men. Only about 20,000 reached their destination and laid siege to the Holy City. Their opponents were divided and demoralized, but the walls of Jerusalem were strong and difficult to breach. Godfrey of Bouillon, the commander of the Crusaders, attacked the city walls from the two sides where there were no deep ravines to protect the city. They attacked on the north side near Herod's Gate and on the south side on Mount Zion. They raised siege towers at the point of attack and, from the top of the siege towers, bridged the walls. After thirty-seven days of siege, the defenders surrendered, on July 15, 1099, and the victors unleashed an indiscriminate massacre of Moslems and Jews. The ruthless scenes of carnage and butchery have been recorded by Christian chroniclers with great delight. The bloody celebration was duly reported to the Pope. "And if you desire to know what was done with the enemy who were found there, know that in Solomon's Porch and in his Temple our men rode in the blood of the Saracens up to the knees of their horses."[2] The Jews of Jerusalem were exterminated in one swoop. They were hounded into a synagogue and the synagogue was set on

2. Quoted in Strayer, Joseph R. and Munro, Dana C., *The Middle Ages 395–1500* (New York, Appleton-Century-Crofts, Inc., 1942), p. 228.

fire. The Jewish Quarter, which was then north of the Temple Mount, where the Moslem Quarter is now located, was burned down. There are sources that tell of Jews having been ransomed from the Crusaders. In all probability, some also escaped together with the Egyptian garrison that was permitted to withdraw to Ascalon. But Jerusalem did become *Judenrein*, as it also became *Moslemrien*—"a city fit for Christian habitation."

After the appalling massacre of Moslems and Jews—according to some, nearly 40,000 men, women, and children—the Crusader barons washed their hands and feet, laid aside their bloodstained clothes for fresh robes, and made their way barefoot to the Church of the Holy Sepulchre where, according to William of Tyre, they shed tears "of joy and pity. . . . They felt as if they had entered into Paradise."[3]

After their service of penitence and adoration at the Holy Sepulchre, the Crusaders began their work in making Jerusalem a place fit for Christians to live in. The dead bodies were removed from the narrow streets and were buried outside the walls. The Church of the Holy Sepulchre was cleansed and mosques were converted into churches, including the Al-Aqsa Mosque. The shrine of the Dome of the Rock was also consecrated to Christian use. They built an altar on the sacred Rock and placed on it a large, gold-plated cross. They also painted some frescoes on the walls and renamed the building the Temple of Solomon. They did not efface the anti-Christian inscriptions. This beautiful mosaic was saved from mutilation not because the Crusaders admired the graceful elegance of the inscription, but because they could not read Arabic and did not take the trouble to have the inscription read to them.

---

3. Quoted in Oldenberg, Zoe, *The Crusades* (New York, Ballantine Books, 1967), p. 167.

When the religious fervor and the war frenzy abated, the conquerors turned their energies to the prosaic details of day-to-day living, and their leaders set out to establish governments suitable for their newly won territories.

It is claimed that nineteen languages were spoken in the First Crusader army. But many of the leaders, including Godfrey of Bouillon, the commander of the siege of Jerusalem, were of French origin. Pope Urban II, who had preached the Crusade, was also of French origin. French, therefore, became the official language of what was to emerge as the Kingdom of Jerusalem, and to this day, Moslems call Westerners "Franks."

The governments that were instituted were feudal in organization, patterned on those current in the West. Barons and lords held their lands as feudatories of a king to whom they swore allegiance. The lords, in turn, parcelled out some of their lands as fiefs to knights who swore allegiance to their lords. The lords owed their king a quota of knights and foot soldiers whenever the king needed them for a campaign.

Theoretically, the king was at the peak of the feudal structure. Actually, his power was nominal, the most powerful barons in his realm having wide political and judicial powers and almost total autonomy.

This loose feudal structure was now imposed upon the alien Eastern soil of their conquests, with Godfrey of Bouillon chosen as the first ruler of the most southern territory: Jerusalem. Of all the leaders of the Crusade, he was the fittest, perhaps the inevitable choice. But he was not king. He refused the crown on the grounds that Jesus had been crowned in Jerusalem with a crown of thorns. How could he wear a crown of gold? He adopted the title of Defender of the Holy Sepulchre. The title of king would have to wait for his successor.

Actually, Godfrey of Bouillon and his successors had governmental problems far more complicated than those mandated by the feudal structure described above. There were many autonomous jurisdictions within the Kingdom: religious military orders such as the Knights Templars; local towns which enjoyed self-government; and the trading colonies of Venice, Genoa, and other trading republics. There was a diversity of religious sects, each with its own governing body. There was no permanent army. Crusaders, feeling that they had fulfilled their religious duty, would pull up stakes and go back home. Replacements would come from the West, only to return in due course. There never were enough available soldiers. And then there was the Patriarch.

In the year 451 c.e., at the Council of Chalcedon, the bishop of Jerusalem had been recognized as a Patriarch, one of the supreme prelates of the Church, coequal with the Patriarchs of Constantinople, Alexandria, Antioch, and Rome. With the Moslem conquests of the Middle East, the Patriarchs of Jerusalem, Alexandria, and Antioch lost a large part of their autonomy. They were appointed by Constantinople and under its religious authority. The bishop of Rome—now known as the Pope, the head of Western Christianity—and the Patriarch of Constantinople, the head of the Eastern Church, were the two poles of the Christian world. And for centuries, the poles had been drifting apart. In 1054 c.e. came the break, known as the Great Schism, with the papal legate, Cardinal Humbert, excommunicating the Patriarch of Constantinople and his followers.

The point of all this being that the Patriarch of Jerusalem was Greek Orthodox while the Crusaders were Roman Catholic. Had a Patriarch been in office at the time, some sort of religious accommodation might have been reached. But, as luck would have it, the Patriarch of Jerusalem, Symeon, had recently died, and no other prelate had been elected to fill his place. The Crusader barons looked upon this vacant office as they looked upon the vacant palaces and towers they had captured: loot to be distributed. In December 1099, they elected Daimbert, Archbishop of Pisa, as Patriarch of Jerusalem. Mindful of the Crusade as a religious endeavor, the new Patriarch now claimed Jerusalem for the Catholic Church, and persuaded Godfrey to accept his realm in fief as a vassal of the Church. This transferring of allegiance from Constantinople to Rome was something the Greek Orthodox clergy and laity, who were the overwhelming majority of the Christian population of the Crusader states, would never forget nor forgive.

With the election of Godfrey as Defender of the Holy Sepulchre and Daimbert as Patriarch of Jerusalem, the Latin (or Roman Catholic) Kingdom of Jerusalem was launched. Theoretically, the principalities of Antioch, Tripoli, and Edessa were subject to Jerusalem. Actually, these principalities were not only independent, but often defied the king of Jerusalem and pursued policies harmful to their theoretical chief.[4]

Godfrey ruled only one year. He died in 1100 and was buried in the Church of the Holy Sepulchre. During that year, he met a large Moslem force, fought a decisive battle near Ascalon, and saved the newly established Crusader Kingdom.

At the time of Godfrey's death, the Kingdom of Jerusalem consisted of only Jerusalem, the port of Jaffa, and about twenty villages. No effective control was exercised over the territory between Jerusalem, its port of Jaffa, and the villages. But Godfrey had inspired fear in the enemy, and several Moslem princes had not only ceded territory to Godfrey but also paid him tribute.

Baldwin, Godfrey's brother, was chosen to be the second ruler. Unlike Godfrey, Baldwin did not reject the crown.

---

4. For a brief but excellent description of the feudal system in the Kingdom of Jerusalem, see G.A. Campbell, *The Knights Templars* (London: Duckworth, 1937), Chapter 6.

His coronation as King of Jerusalem was accompanied by scenes of splendor characteristic of the East. He adopted Eastern dress and manners, and his court was that of an oriental ruler.

Baldwin reigned from 1100 to 1118. He was constantly engaged in wars for which he had but few soldiers. In desperation, Baldwin resorted to pressing the pilgrims into army service. Yet he succeeded in extending the Kingdom's territory to include the coastal towns of Caesarea, Haifa, Acre, Sidon, and Beirut. These conquests were made possible by the assistance of the Venetian, Genoan, and other European maritime republics' fleets.

During the reign of Baldwin II, who ascended the throne in 1118, the Latin Kingdom of Jerusalem attained its greatest extent. By the end of his reign, the Christian dominion extended from the Mediterranean Sea to the Arabian desert and from Ascalon to Beirut.

When the Crusaders captured Jerusalem, the influx of pilgrims increased. However, many of the pilgrims arrived in Jerusalem in a sorry condition. Some arrived in a state of destitution because they had been robbed on the way to the Holy City. Others arrived sick or wounded in conflicts with Arab robber bands. The pilgrims were in desperate need of help. This led to the founding of military orders whose declared duty it was to defend the pilgrims against the Moslem robber bands and to care for their sick and wounded. The Templars and Hospitallers are the best known of these orders.

The Hospitallers were the first order to be founded in Jerusalem, and they were centered in the Hospital of St. John. The members took the triple vow of obedience, chastity, and poverty. They also vowed to devote themselves to the ailing and the needy, and to renounce worldly pleasure. At first, the Hospitallers carried out their vows in an exemplary manner, and they were praised by all who came into contact with them. As a result, many endowments and cash income flowed into the order's coffers. In 1113, the Pope accorded them the privilege of electing their leaders without reference to the Church authorities in Jerusalem. This gave the order independence from all ecclesiastical or lay authority, except that of the Pope.

There was still need of an organization to protect the pilgrims on their long trek to Jerusalem. The success of the Hospitallers encouraged the founding of the Knights Templars, who dedicated themselves to the protection of the pilgrims against the Moslem robber bands. In 1118, nine knights organized themselves to perform the service of guiding and guarding the pilgrims. From this small beginning developed the powerful order which, after more than two centuries of distinguished service, became so powerful as to become a threat to the Vatican itself.

The Templars also took the oath of obedience, chastity, and poverty, and they, too, soon gained a reputation as successful guides and protectors of the pilgrims; this, despite their being so few. The founding few were given a dwelling on the Temple Mount near the Dome of the Rock or, as the Crusaders called it, *Templum Domini*. From this location of their dwelling, they derived their name: the Knights Templars. In 1124, they appropriated the Al-Aqsa Mosque. They also appropriated the so-called Solomon's Stables under the Mosque and actually used them as stables for their horses.

Although the Templars had been organized to guide and protect the pilgrims, they soon assumed the added function of fighting the infidel per se. They thus became the nucleus of an army dedicated to perpetual war with Islam. Although they were sworn servants of the Church, their central duty was not to minister as priests or to live as monks, but to fight the infidels. This dual function of being both monks and warriors was new in Christendom.

The Templars' reputation as men who were valiant in war and pious servants of the Church spread widely and their popularity grew. Voluntary offerings flowed into their coffers, and recruits swelled their ranks.

As the Templars became rich and powerful, they ceased to be docile servants of the Church of Jerusalem. In 1128, the Knights Templars became an independent order responsible only to the Pope. Their property endowments in Europe increased, and their power spread far beyond the Holy Land. It was estimated that, in the thirteenth century, the Templars' income from their vast estates in Europe was six million pounds annually. The Templars' wealth aroused the envy of Church and State. Their preceptors, who were in charge of their property in various parts of Europe, also recruited, housed, trained, and shipped new recruits to Jerusalem, where they became religious knights of the Temple.

The Hospitallers emulated the younger order and, in 1153, officially became a fighting brotherhood. They, too, undertook to defend the Christian kingdom against the Moslem infidels. As a result, they, too, waxed rich and powerful. The two fighting orders were often in competition for recruits. They often schemed against each other and, at times, even followed contradictory policies aimed at weakening each other.

As the power of the military orders grew, they began to defy the Patriarch of Jerusalem. In 1179, and again in 1186, the Pope rebuked the orders for the highhanded defiance of the Church of Jerusalem. However, they continued to be the core of the military power of the Latin Kingdom of Jerusalem. They served as an effective standing army, always ready to respond to a call to arms in defense of the Kingdom of Jerusalem. The orders also built fortresses at strategic points along the borders. These strongholds also provided a refuge for the Christian population in their vicinity in time of danger. The knights and their supporting infantry, consisting of their retainers—six foot soldiers to every knight—constituted the offensive and defensive force of the Crusader Kingdom.

The fame of the Crusaders as energetic and masterly builders has surpassed their glory as warriors. They engaged in a vast building program, dotting the country with churches, convents, hospices, and residences for clergy. As feudal chiefs, they also built for themselves luxurious palaces which, in time, served not merely as residences, but also as seats of power, luxury, and lust. The most important of their building enterprises was the reconstruction of the Church of the Holy Sepulchre. When the Crusaders rebuilt the Martyrion, they did not make it a separate building, as Constantine had done, but they connected it with the Anastasis, taking in the open court that had separated these two main buildings. This new structure enclosed all the holy places that had grown up around the original two church buildings. The separate churches that had clustered around the Anastasis now became small chapels around the Holy Sepulchre, and the Golgotha Church now became a mezzanine floor in the new building. Thus, the Church of the Holy Sepulchre, in its present form, came into being. It took the Crusaders twenty years to complete the structure. The dedication of the new church took place on July 15, 1149, which coincided with the fiftieth anniversary of the capture of Jerusalem by Godfrey of Bouillon. Another important church structure in Jerusalem that was erected by the Crusaders was the Church of St. Anne. This church is regarded by many as a perfect example of Crusader architecture.

The Crusaders are remembered for the fortresses and towers they built at many strategic points. But they did not build city walls because they did not have the manpower for the defense of long walls. Instead, they strengthened the castles that most towns had. The Crusader castles were almost impregnable, and they were provisioned to withstand an enemy siege for years. The advantage of a castle is

that it can be held against a large army by a mere few
hundred defenders. The only city walls the Crusaders built
were the walls of Jerusalem. They restored the walls,
following the lines of the Roman walls of Aelia Capitolina.
Hence, the part of Mount Zion in which were located the
Coenaculum and King David's Tomb were once more
outside the walls.

The Crusader architecture exerted an influence over
future generations. It is distinctive, and one can easily
recognize the typical Crusader capitals, their slanting
window sills, and their characteristic cornices. They made
extensive use of the frill which enabled them not only to
make holes in the stone, but also to make free standing
decorative parts in a stone capital. Many examples of this
Crusader architectural technique can now be seen in the
Church of the Holy Sepulchre.

The quality of the Crusader structure is highly admired
to this day. George Adam Smith exclaims:

> How firmly they built! Today the mortar in their castles is
> harder than the stone it binds. But it is not by these coast
> fortresses, nor by the huge castles crowning the heights far
> inland, that the Crusaders impress you, so much as by the
> ruins of lonely churches and cloisters, which are scattered
> all over the land, far from the coast and the shelter of the
> great Frankish citadels.[5]

The strength and durability of a nation cannot be measured by its buildings, be they military or religious. The
determining factors are such intangibles as the people's
moral and spiritual fiber. By these standards, the Crusader
kingdom was wanting. The vices of the East proved more
powerful enemies than the hostile armies which were poised

---

5. George Adam Smith, *The Historical Geography of the Holy Land*,
14th ed. (New York: A.C. Armstrong, 1908), 39.

against them. Degeneration rapidly followed the Crusaders' initial success. Luxury and sloth became acceptable ways of life. Drunken orgies and gambling were usual forms of entertainment, and the courts of the nobles could vie in their splendor with those of European kings. Even unnatural vices, not uncommon in the East, were adopted by the Crusaders, even in the ranks of the leaders.

Nor can the initial success in expanding the territorial dimensions of the Kingdom be a measure of national strength. Baldwin, the second Crusader king, did extend the boundaries of the realm, but he did not achieve reconciliation between the Eastern and Western Churches. Byzantium, the Eastern Church, continued to see, in the Crusaders, a threat to its security and remained unfriendly. The Eastern clergy were disillusioned by the conduct of the Latin priests. Neither did the Crusaders succeed in converting the Moslems to Christianity.

But the main weakness of the Crusader Kingdom was its scanty population. The capture of Jerusalem aroused great enthusiasm all over Christian Europe. But the men of the crusade were leaving for their homes in Europe. They had achieved their goal and felt free to return to their normal vocations. Only 300 knights and about 2,000 foot soldiers remained. The Holy City was only a city of ecclesiastics, pilgrims, troops, and the civilians who served them. During the pilgrim seasons, the streets and the bazaars filled up. Otherwise, the permanent Christian population was small and did not expand. The shortage of manpower plagued the Kingdom of Jerusalem all the years of its existence. In their desperation, the kings were liberal to immigrants. They welcomed "heretical" Christians and even Jews. Moslems were not molested. They, too, could be counted as subjects.

The small Christian population also lost the vigor and energy that had characterized the first settlers. The second and third generations who grew up in the land sought luxury and pleasure. The Kingdom of Jerusalem survived only because of the religious orders whose courage and daring were exemplary. They always responded to the call to arms, and fought heroically. They were said to have fought at odds of 20-to-one and prevailed. At first, the knights in massive armor, mounted and well-trained, were superior to the light Moslem cavalry. However, the Templars and Hospitallers were only a skeleton of an army. Demoralization manifested itself in direct proportion to the growth of their wealth and power. While they continued to be brave on the field of battle, they also became ridden with greed, lust, and treachery. This demoralization is fully recorded in their chronicles. And eventually the Saracens developed mobile tactics which succeeded in overcoming the Crusaders' initial advantage. The days of the Crusader Kingdom of Jerusalem were numbered.[6]

---

6. The Templars were disbanded by the Pope. The charges of corruption and immorality shocked both laity and clergy. Some have questioned the motives of the accusers. But there was much truth in the accusations. After the fall of the Kingdom of Jerusalem, the Hospitallers transferred their headquarters to Rhodes, where they became the rulers of a territorial state. When the Turks captured Rhodes in 1522, Emperor Charles V ceded them the island of Malta. The Hospitallers are now generally called the Knights of Malta. Their decline began with the rise of the Reformation, and Napoleon hastened the process when he conquered the island in 1798. The order still exists and its headquarters are in Rome.

11

The Fall of the Latin Kingdom of Jerusalem

The first convincing sign of the approaching fall of the Latin Kingdom of Jerusalem was a decisive battle in 1144, only 45 years after the Crusaders had captured Jerusalem. In that battle, one of the Crusaders' principalities, the County of Edessa, was overrun by the Moslems. This was the turning point in the war between the East and the West. From then on, the power of the Christians waned steadily.

This stunning defeat aroused the European Christians and the Second Crusade was launched in 1146. The aim of this Crusade was to recapture Edessa and to strengthen the Crusader holdings in the East. But this Crusade was a total fiasco because of ineptitude and treachery. The only effect this Crusade had on the situation in the Holy Land was to encourage Moslem hopes of sweeping the Franks from their kingdoms. The man who led the Moslems in the "sweeping" operation was a Kurd by the name of *Salah ed-din*, generally known as *Saladin*.

Saladin became the ruler of Egypt in 1171. While Saladin's power was waxing, that of the Latin Kingdom of Jerusalem was definitely waning. The military orders were quarreling with each other. They were united only in their contempt for the secular and religious rulers in the Kingdom. No help was in sight from Europe, and many Christians were leaving in anticipation of the Moslem victory.

Saladin was the most formidable enemy that the Latin Kingdom of Jerusalem had faced in the seventy-five years of its existence. Saladin bore down on the Crusader Kingdom from all sides. The Crusaders chalked up to their credit several resounding victories, but the ultimate outcome was predictable. Saladin marched for the decisive battle with an army of 80,000 men; the Christians rallied an army of only 15,000, of whom only 1,200 were knights. At the Horns of Hattin, which is located between Tiberius and Nazareth, the armies were locked in fateful battle. The Crusaders fought bravely to the end, but they were impeded by their heavy armor which proved a hindrance in the hilly country. In addition, there was, at the time, a fierce sirocco, which roasted the men inside their metal armor. The scrub caught fire in the heat, and the fire flaming into their faces proved most distressing. Many a knight was literally smothered in his metal armor. Topping these most disastrous conditions was a lack of water to quench the men's intolerable thirst. The outcome of the battle was a stunning victory for Saladin. Of an army of 15,000 Christian soldiers, only one thousand escaped death or slavery. The Crusaders also lost the fragment of the True Cross which they had carried into battle, hoping that the holy relic would bring them victory. The King of Jerusalem was taken captive. So were the Masters of the Templars and the Hospitallers. Since the Christians had mobilized their total manpower for this battle, there were no reserves available for the defense of the land. The fate of the

Kingdom of Jerusalem was sealed. The Crusader castles, being practically unmanned, fell easily to the Moslems. The same fate awaited Jerusalem. Saladin laid siege to the Holy City and, within two weeks, the city surrendered. Saladin did not massacre the inhabitants. Instead, he collected a ransom of ten Tyrian dinars for each man, five dinars for each woman, and one dinar for each child. The poorer Christians who could not produce the fees were sold into slavery. There were some additional terms which were humiliating but not fatal to the Christians or to Christianity. "On the very day of capitulation," writes Saladin's biographer, Beha ed-din, "Friday's prayer was solemnized in the city, and Khatib delivered the sermon.[1] The huge cross that rose from the dome of the *Sakhra* was thrown down. In this manner, by means of the Sultan, God accorded a magnificent triumph to Islam."[2] Saladin expelled the Latins, but the Eastern Christians he allowed to remain in the city. Historians usually contrast the relative humanitarian conduct of the Moslems when they entered Jerusalem with the massive slaughter of the Moslem and Jewish populations when the Crusaders entered the Holy City. While the Crusaders waded "knee-deep" in the blood of their victims, Saladin was comparatively magnanimous. Like Omar, he granted his erstwhile enemies safety of life and property. To be sure, Saladin converted most of the churches into mosques, but he spared the lives of the Christians and permitted them to leave the city for safer areas. George Williams describes the event:

---

1. An English translation of Khatib's sermon will be found in *Ibn Khallikan's Biographical Dictionary*, trans. Mac Guckin de Slane (Paris: Oriental Translation Fund of Great Britain and Ireland, 1843), 634–641.

2. Beha Ed-din, "The Life of Saladin," *Palestine Pilgrims' Text Society: The Library*, Vol. 13 (London: Committee of the Palestine Exploration Fund, 1897): 119–120.

The dismay of Christendom at the fall of Jerusalem was equalled only by the joy of the Moslems at its recovery, which they celebrated with all imaginable tokens of gratitude. The Koran was restored to the pulpit, the voices of the Muezzin again called to prayer, the mosques rang with the shout of victory and the confession of Islam. The Noble Rock was disencumbered from its abominations, and extreme was the horror of the Moslems to discover that it had suffered diminution by violence. The walls and pavement were purified from Christian defilement with rosewater from Damascus; the golden cross, torn from its height to be replaced by the crescent, was dragged in dishonor through the streets, amid the triumphant exultation of the Moslems; while the weeping Christians tore their hair, beat their breasts, and rent their garments at the heart-rending sight of such awful desecration! The lodging of the Templars on the west of Al-Aqsa, with their granaries and offices, were removed, all things were restored to their former condition, and the mosks richly furnished with lamps and carpets.[3]

Saladin arranged for the burial of his heroic followers on the eastern side of the Temple Mount where many other famous Moslems were interred. He also turned St. Anne's Church into a *madrassah* for religious studies, and caused Islamic learning to be resumed. Since the Church of the Holy Sepulchre is not a Moslem holy place, Saladin merely transferred it to the Greek Orthodox Church. Ever since then, except for the fifteen years, from 1229 to 1244, when Jerusalem was again under Crusader control, the main basilica of the Church of the Holy Sepulchre has been the cathedral of the Greek Patriarchs.

Saladin also permitted the Jews to settle in Jerusalem.

---

3. George Williams, *The Holy City: Historical, Topographical, and Antiquarian Notices of Jerusalem*, 2d ed., Vol. 1 (London: Parker, 1849), 418.

He thus endeared himself to Jewish memory. The Spanish-Jewish poet al-Harizi wrote in 1216:

> Saladin ordered to proclaim in every city, to let it be known to old and young; Speak ye to the heart of Jerusalem, let anybody from the seed of Ephraim, who wants, come to her.[4]

De facto, the Latin Kingdom of Jerusalem ceased to be. It had lasted from 1099 to 1187, less than ninety years. Despite Jerusalem's return to Christian rule for fifteen years, between 1229 and 1244, the year 1187 is, for all practical purposes, the year when Jerusalem once more became a Moslem city, and so it remained for over 700 years.

Christians in the European states were shocked by the fall of Jerusalem. The Pope imposed a penance on all Christians to fast on the sixth day of the week and on the fourth day "to abstain from eating flesh." A Third Crusade was launched. The exploits of Saladin and Richard I, "the Lion Hearted," have been romanticized in literature. However, as far as Jerusalem was concerned, these battles were not decisive. The Third Crusade also ended without freeing Jerusalem from the Moslems.

Saladin died in 1193. Though his successors were not as formidable, Jerusalem was not reconquered by the Christians. A Fourth Crusade was launched, but it spent itself in a war on Constantinople. Crusade after Crusade followed, ending mainly as fiascoes because of divided counsel and keen jealousies among the leaders.

The passage from Christianity to Islam was accomplished in a very short time. This rapid displacement of Christianity by Islam was due, in large measure, to the

---

4. Quoted in Joshua Prawer, *The Latin Kingdom of Jerusalem* (London: Weidenfeld and Nicolson Ltd., 1972), 244.

moral state of the contending forces. The people in the Holy Land associated Christianity with the Christian kings and nobles in whose conduct they saw only luxury, corruption, and vice. In the Moslem leaders, they saw simple, austere, and religious men. The Moslem leaders also appeared to be tolerant. These spiritual qualities did not endure for long, least of all the seeming tolerance. But at the outset, the contrast was vivid and convincing. Many Christians received the Moslem conquerors with joy, only to discover later that the Moslems could be intolerant to the point of forcing a change of faith on some of their subjects. The remnant of the Christians were settled in the mountains of Lebanon. Some were suffered to remain in Jerusalem near the Church of the Holy Sepulchre and in Bethlehem near the Church of the Nativity.

The Crusader zeal had not yet spent itself completely. In a last gasp, it managed to return to Jerusalem, not under the auspices of the Church, nor by appeal to arms, but by shrewd political maneuvers.

Frederick II, Emperor of Germany, had repeatedly pledged to go on a Crusade. Each time he reneged on his pledge. This brought down the wrath of the Pope upon him, and he was excommunicated. The anathema forced him to act, even in the face of papal opposition. He, therefore, proceeded on a Crusade of his own.[5] He landed in Acre in September 1228 with an army of 30,000. Instead of going into battle, he entered into negotiations with the Moslems who were then engaged in an internecine war. In 1229, Frederick signed a treaty with the Sultan of Egypt who

---

5. Among those who joined Frederick on his strange Crusade was one of the signers of the Magna Carta, Philip d'Aubigny, who had also been tutor to King Henry III. Philip d'Aubigny died in Jerusalem in 1236 and was buried near the main portal of the Church of the Holy Sepulchre. His burial place was discovered when an old stone platform, used by the Turkish doorkeepers, was removed.

ceded to Frederick the cities of Jerusalem, Jaffa, Bethlehem, and Nazareth. This was a remarkable achievement. The Kingdom of Jerusalem was restored without a single blow, in the face of papal opposition, and by one who was under the ban of excommunication. The treaty was for ten years; it provided that the Temple Mount with its Dome of the Rock and the Al-Aqsa Mosque were to remain under Moslem jurisdiction. This, however, was a minor consideration. The Latin Kingdom of Jerusalem was again a reality, and Frederick, the excommunicate, entered the Church of the Holy Sepulchre to be crowned King of Jerusalem. In obedience to papal orders, not a single priest was present. So Frederick crowned himself. He appointed a viceroy and left to attend to urgent matters at home.

Intrigues and shrewd diplomacy expanded the realm of the Latin Kingdom so that by 1240 the area of the Kingdom included the coastal strip from Beirut to Gaza, Galilee, and Judea up to, but not including, Hebron. Even the Temple Mount was ceded to Frederick's Latin Kingdom of Jerusalem. These gains were achieved by switching the alliance from Egypt to Damascus.

Aggrieved, Egypt reacted to this diplomatic duplicity by inviting in the Khorasmian Turks, a wild Tartar horde who had broken away from the Mongols. The Khorasmians invaded the land and laid it waste. They captured Jerusalem, massacred an estimated 20,000 people, and plundered the churches, including the Church of the Holy Sepulchre. In their search for treasure, they desecrated the tombs of Godfrey and Baldwin inside the Church of the Holy Sepulchre. In 1244, a decisive battle was fought near Gaza. The Crusaders suffered a crushing defeat at the hands of a combined force of Egyptians and Khorasmians. In this battle, the Khorasmian Turks exhausted themselves. In 1247, the Egyptians attacked these invaders and decimated them. The remnants of the Khorasmians withdrew from the land.

Thus ended the strange episode of the Second Latin Kingdom of Jerusalem. This fifteen-year interlude was of little historic significance. As already stated, for all practical considerations, Christian rule in Jerusalem had ended with Saladin's victory in 1187. Long, barren centuries of Saracen and Turkish rule now followed, not to be ended till the British captured Jerusalem on December 10, 1917.

12

Jerusalem Under the Mamelukes

Shortly after the breakup of the Second Crusader Kingdom, the Mamelukes came to power in Egypt, and they ruled Egypt and its dependencies, including Jerusalem, for more than two-and-a-half centuries.

The word Mameluke means slave; the Mameluke Sultans were Egyptian rulers who had been slaves. They were purchased in their childhood from their parents who were mostly Circassians or Turks. These children were converted to Islam and then trained to be professional soldiers. From their ranks came their officers. This system was introduced in Egypt in order to develop a professional army with no family connections or loyalties. The Sultan could rely on these soldiers not only on the battlefield but also within the realm. The system was a great success. The Mamelukes, as a military force, were feared. They were competent and brave, and their loyalty to the Sultan was absolute. These Mamelukes were also very loyal to each other. Having no family, they accepted each other as brothers. But the inevitable happened. A very able and ambitious Mameluke general toppled a weak Sultan and ascended the throne. Since only Mamelukes could now be Sultans, no dynasty could be established because the son of a Sultan had never been a slave. Each new Sultan was, therefore, chosen from among the Mameluke generals in the army. The Mameluke Sultans were, as a rule, gifted military leaders, and they continued to govern Egypt, as noted above, for two and a half centuries.

It was in 1250 that a Mameluke general named Baibars overthrew the Caliphate and became the Sultan of Egypt. Thus Jerusalem came to be ruled by the Mamelukes. As a warrior, Sultan Baibars is remembered especially for his campaign against the Mongols who had invaded the Holy Land and laid it waste.

The Mongol invasion in 1260 was one of the most devastating events in the history of Jerusalem. This disastrous event is hardly noticed by many historians because, no sooner was Jerusalem conquered by the Mongols, than they withdrew. The devastation, however, was overwhelming. One can gauge the effect of this disaster by the statement of the famous Jewish scholar Nachmanides that he found, in the city, a population of only 2,000. In view of the fact that the population of Jerusalem had been previously estimated at about 30,000, one can readily grasp the devastation left by the Mongols. Baibars met the Mongols in a decisive battle near what is now Ein Harod. He defeated them and freed the land of that scourge.

In 1291, one of Baibar's successors, the Sultan al-Ashraf Khalil, defeated the last of the Crusader kingdoms in the Holy Land, the Kingdom of Acre. That ended the Crusader episode. The Mamelukes were now in full control of the Holy Land. In order to prevent a return of the Christians, all Crusader castles and fortresses were destroyed. So were the coastal cities. This "scorched earth" policy was aimed at making it impossible for another Crusader army to land on the coast of the Holy Land.

Although Jerusalem was a holy city for the Moslems, it was treated by the Mameluke Sultans as a "remote" provincial town of little military value. The city was governed from a provincial capital, which, at one time, was Gaza. As a result, Jerusalem suffered from neglect and misgovernment. The walls were in ruins, and the city was exposed to frequent raids by roving Arab bands. Those who were attached to the holy places stayed and suffered, and the small civilian population lived in fear and poverty. While Alexandria rose as an international port, the coastal cities of the Holy Land were almost idle. Few pilgrims came to Jaffa, because the tolls and bribes imposed on them were excessive. Non-Moslems, both Christians and Jews, found life difficult because of extortions by local officials. In 1382, the Mamelukes began to enforce distinctive headgear for the infidels so that the Moslems, who wore white turbans, might identify the infidels. Jews had to wear yellow turbans and Christians blue turbans.

The Mamelukes were extensive builders, and Jerusalem benefited from their architectural interest. The Mamelukes rebuilt the Citadel and gave it its present form. They repaired the water-supply system and water again flowed from Solomon's Pools in the Hebron Hills of Jerusalem. More impressive for Jerusalem's architectural appearance were the religious buildings and the private dwellings that the Mamelukes erected in the city. Among those responsible for much of the Mameluke building activity in Jerusalem were a number of banished dignitaries who lived in Jerusalem. Since Jerusalem was regarded by the Mameluke Sultans as a remote provincial town, they made it a practice to banish discredited dignitaries to Jerusalem. Thus is happened that there was in Jerusalem a colony of exiled generals and other high government officials. These wealthy Mamelukes built and endowed mosques, madrassahs, and hostels for Moslem scholars and mystics. They also added a string of Moslem structures on the Temple Mount. Among these were cloisters, several beautiful arches, and four elegant minarets. Not to be overlooked were the palatial homes that they fashioned for themselves. The masonry of alternating red and white stone, and their stalactite semi-domes are still a feature of many old buildings in Jerusalem.

One of the pilgrims who visited Jerusalem in 1483 was a monk, Brother Felix Fabri. He bewailed the fact that things were not what they used to be "in the good old times," that is, in the days of the Crusader Kingdom, when the Latins were in control. He wrote in his itinerary:

> The Church of the Holy Sepulchre is more beautiful than all the other churches in the world . . . yet it is rendered hideous and shocking by the abominable errors of those who enter it. In the good old times Christians from all parts of the world, and speaking all languages, used to enter it, desiring to worship God, without any errors, treacheries, or superstitions, while excommunicated persons, schismatics, and outcast heretics, of whom, alas! the temple is now full, by whom the holy building is defiled, were then denied admittance.[1]

What bothered the good monk was that Moslem rule in Jerusalem led to the decline of the Western Latin Church and the corresponding ascendance of the Greek Orthodox Church. The Eastern Church was now in control of the most important holy places, especially the Holy Sepulchre. "In the good old times" when the Crusaders ruled Jerusalem, things were different. Now the Eastern Church re-

---

1. Felix Fabri, "The Wanderings of Felix Fabri," trans. Aubrey Stewart, *Palestine Pilgrims' Text Society: The Library*, Vol. 3 (London: Committee of the Palestine Exploration Fund, 1896): 430–431.

gained its former prestige, while the Latin Patriarchate fell into abeyance. Moreover, the custody of the keys to the Church of the Holy Sepulchre were now entrusted to two Moslem families. The descendents of one of these families still retain the privilege of keeping the keys, and the descendents of the other family retain the privilege of opening the Church for Christian worship.

During the Mameluke period, the Georgians were granted rights to a number of important holy places. The Georgians were known as brave soldiers, and their land in the Caucasus was strategically located. Their good will was courted. Hence they were favored by the Mameluke Sultans and were granted religious privileges. The Georgians owned the Monastery of the Cross, Calvary inside the Church of the Holy Sepulchre, and several other holy places. In later years, poverty forced them to transfer these precious possessions to the Greek Orthodox Church.

The Latins did not abandon their privileges with resignation. They persisted in their efforts to regain their standing in Jerusalem. The Latins were fortunate in having the Franciscan Order as custodians of their holy places. The Order was founded by St. Francis of Assisi at the beginning of the thirteenth century. After their founder had visited the Holy Land, the Franciscans followed and established themselves as custodians of the Latin holy places. In 1342, Pope Clemens VI officially invested the Order with the responsibility of guarding the holy places. When the Latin Patriarchate fell into abeyance, the Franciscans assumed the responsibility for the Western Church, and the head of the Franciscan Order in Jerusalem became the *Padre Custode di Terra Santa*—the Father *custos* of the Holy Land. The Franciscans have dedicated themselves to their sacred tasks with selfless devotion and have carried out their duties with dedication and success.

When the Second Latin Kingdom fell in 1291, the Franciscans were expelled from the Holy Land. They returned in 1335 and settled on Mount Zion. The Coenaculum was ceded to them, and, in time, they also acquired rights in the Church of the Holy Sepulchre as well as the full possession of the Sepulchre of the Virgin Mary. The Franciscans established hospices for pilgrims and at all times performed their duties at the holy places meticulously.

Saladin and his successors, the Mamelukes, allowed the Jews to return to Jerusalem. The Jewish scholar al-Harizi (1170–1235) reports that 300 rabbis from France and England came to the Holy Land in 1211. However, the effective resettlement of Jews in Jerusalem did not begin till the arrival, in 1267, of the renowned scholar Rabbi Moses ben Nachman, generally called by the initial letters of his name, the **RaMBaN** or Nachmanides. In a letter to his son in Spain the scholar wrote:

> But what shall I say to you concerning the country? Great is the solitude and great the devastation, and, to put it briefly, the more sacred the places, the greater their desolation. Jerusalem is more desolate than the rest of the country: Judaea more than Galilee. But even in this destruction it is a blessed land. It has about 2,000 inhabitants; about 300 Christians live there who escaped the sword of the Sultan. There are no more Jews. For, after the arrival of the Tartars, some fled while others died by the sword. There are only two brothers, dyers by trade, who have to buy their ingredients from the government. There the Ten Men[2] meet, and on Sabbaths they hold the service at their home. But we encouraged them, and we succeeded in finding a vacant house, built on pillars of marble with a beautiful arch. That we took for a synagogue. For the town is without a ruler, so that whoever desires to take possession of the ruins can do so. We gave our offering towards the repairs of the house. We have sent already to Shechem (Nablus) to

---

2. Ten Men are needed for a Jewish congregation to hold a service.

fetch some scrolls of the Law which had been brought thither from Jerusalem on the invasion of the Tartars. Thus they will organize a synagogue and worship there. For, continually people crowd into Jerusalem, men and women, from Damascus, Zobah (Aleppo), and from all parts of the country, to see the Sanctuary and to mourn there.[3]

After the Mongol invasion the city was so depopulated that anyone could take possession of abandoned buildings. The building that the Ramban acquired became the first Sephardi house of prayer in Jerusalem in the post-Crusader period. With the arrival of the Ramban, Jerusalem became a center of Jewish learning, and Jewish life revolved around the Ramban Synagogue.

The revered Jewish cemetery on the Mount of Olives was already in existence during this period. Jewish graves were located on the eastern slope of the Temple Mount and extended across the Kidron Valley to the slope of the Mount of Olives.

Toward the end of the Mameluke period, the Jewish community was again invigorated by the arrival of a famous scholar, Rabbi Ovadia of Bertinoro (1415–1510). However, there were at that time more powerful historic factors that led to the substantial growth of the Jewish community in Jerusalem. These were the expulsion of the Jews from Spain in 1492, and the conquest of Jerusalem by the Ottoman Turks in 1517. However, the effects of these momentous events on the Jewish community in Jerusalem belong to the next era, the era of the Ottoman Turks.

---

3. Rabbi Moses ben Nachman in *A Treasury of Jewish Letters*, Vol. 1, ed. Franz Kobler (Philadelphia: The Jewish Publication Society, 1953), 226.

13

Turkish Rule in Jerusalem

The Ottoman[1] Turks captured Jerusalem in 1517, and they held on to their prize for 400 years. Their impact on the Holy City, especially during the first three centuries, was minimal. Their reputation as a government has been described as inept, inefficient, and corrupt.

In its heyday, the Ottoman Turkish empire was the greatest military power. The Turks conquered much of southern Europe and even threatened Rome and Vienna. Their power rested largely on a military organization that consisted of professional soldiers known as *Janissaries*. These soldiers were, like the Mamelukes, purchased in their childhood from Christian parents, mainly in the Balkans. They were placed with Moslem families, converted to Islam, and then taken to Constantinople where

---

1. The name is derived from Osman, the name of the original tribe. The Arabs pronounced the word Othman. The Byzantines transformed the word to Ottoman.

they were trained as an elite corps. They took a vow of celibacy and practiced certain religious rites of a rigorous type. During the height of the Ottoman empire, the Janissaries were the most efficient, most cruel, and most feared troops in the world. In the sixteenth century decadence set in. Celibacy was abandoned and ordinary Moslems were admitted into their ranks. They were finally suppressed in 1826.

The Ottoman Turks started out as a religious military organization of Moslem knights who were dedicated to waging an unending war against the Christian infidels. These military units gained popularity and wide support. Recruits came from far and wide. As they met with local success, they set up small states in Asia Minor, which was the area of their concentration. These small principalities served them as centers of power.

Since their goal was to battle the Christians, the Turkish orientation was always European. They had no interest in the Middle East, including the Holy Land, whose inhabitants were mainly Moslem. Turkey has, therefore, regarded itself as a European state.

By 1400, the Turks had overrun Serbia and Bulgaria. They had thus cut off Constantinople from the rest of Europe and doomed the Byzantine empire. The Tartar invasion delayed Constantinople's anticipated doom. In the mid-fifteenth century, Mohammed II, surnamed the Conqueror, led a Turkish army which was superbly organized and expertly trained against Constantinople. The Turkish army was also equipped with heavy artillery. The European armies, however, were still equipped with ineffective catapults. More important, the European nations were unable to unite against the common enemy. In 1453, after a desperate siege, Constantinople fell to the Turks. The Byzantine empire was thus replaced by a strong military power of an alien race and religion. Under Sultan Mohammed II, the Ottomans continued their conquests in Europe and almost achieved their goal of conquering Rome. When the Sultan's grandson, Selim I, ascended the throne in 1512, he found it necessary to turn his eyes to the east and south. This was, however, solely because of imperial necessity. He feared attacks from Persia, Egypt, and even India. He engaged the Persians in battle and defeated them. He then routed the Mamelukes and captured Jerusalem in 1517, practically without resistance. Turkey thus came into possession of Egypt and its dependencies, which included Syria and the Holy Land. When Selim died, he had almost doubled the Turkish deminions, which now included the three Moslem holy cities of Mecca, Medina, and Jerusalem. The Sultan of Turkey thus acquired the title of "Servant and Guardian" of the holy places of Islam. Like Saladin, he repaired the Dome of the Rock, endowed a madrasssah (religious academy), and established hostels for religious mystics.

Selim's successor was his son, Suleiman the Magnificent, who ruled from 1520 to 1566. Since his eastern flank was now secure, he turned back to Europe and undertook a campaign that threatened the heart of the Western continent. He reached Vienna and almost captured it. During the reign of Suleiman the Magnificent, Turkey reached its peak. In Jerusalem, Suleiman left a magnificent memorial, for it was he who rebuilt the city's walls, gates, and towers. The graceful Damascus Gate is a credit to Suleiman's builders. The walls followed the Roman fortifications which had encircled Aelia Capitolina. Most of Mount Zion was thus left outside the city walls. Suleiman's walls have endured from the time they were erected in 1541, and they still stand out as a symbol of Jerusalem's glory. Suleiman also repaired and beautified the Dome of the Rock and restored the aqueducts from Solomon's Pools.

Suleiman's reason for rebuilding the walls of Jerusalem

was not their military value. Cannon had already made
their impact on military tactics, and walls had ceased to be
a protection for a city. However, the walls did protect the
inhabitants from the roving robber bands who plundered
the city's residents almost at will. Jerusalem now had a
measure of peace. The city's main plight, however, derived
chiefly from another source—from government neglect
and misrule.

In the first three hundred years of Turkish rule, Jerusalem practically had no history; that is, nothing seemed to
happen. Only two incidents stand out, one near the beginning of that era and the other at the end. The first has
already been mentioned: the building of the walls around
the city by Sultan Suleiman in 1541. The second was
Napoleon's invasion of the Holy Land and his siege of Acre
in 1799. This invasion, however, had no practical effect on
Jerusalem, for he never got there.

While history seemed to be at a standstill in Jerusalem,
the life and suffering of the inhabitants continued. Pashas
came and went; Jerusalem languished; and corruption
thrived. In the center of Jerusalem's life stood a system of
government which contained the seeds of corruption and
neglect.

The Turks divided the land into districts, each of which
was headed by a governor with absolute power over the
inhabitants. Jerusalem was regarded as a mere provincial
town with little strategic, political, or economic significance. It did not merit the distinction of being the district
capital. Jerusalem was governed by an emissary of the
Pasha whose headquarters were in Damascus. While the
Pasha was away, the local governor was master, and
he ruled despotically. His despotism could be softened only
by handsome bribes.

A governor served only one year. If he were allowed to
stay for a longer period, he might entrench himself and

become a threat to the Sultan. The governor also had to pay in advance to the Sultan's treasury the anticipated taxes of the district. Since Constantinople was always short of money, the anticipated taxes were as high as the market would bear. Under these circumstances, one can readily see the nature of the government in any given district or city. The governor, knowing that he would stay in office only one year, did not take any interest in the city's well-being. Often, he did not even bring his family to the district capital. In addition, the governors were always Turks and therefore felt no affinity to the local population which, in Jerusalem, was mostly Arab and Jewish. The governor therefore had no interest in improving the administration or the living conditions of his district. This accounts for the gross neglect that characterized the Turkish government in the provinces.

The cities deteriorated and wallowed in dirt and disease. But still worse was the fiscal aspect of the governor's rule. Having paid heavily for his post, he was determined to recoup his investment plus a handsome profit. Hence, there was no limit to the governor's extortions from both the laity and the clergy. In short, *bakshish* was the power that turned the wheels of government. Every official expected to be bribed. Hands were always open to receive bakshish.

The government neglect resulted in the general deterioration of the city. Historical monuments were allowed to fall into ruin or to be removed at will for building material. Most discouraging was the hopelessness of the situation. There seemed to be no prospect of any improvement of the city's commerce, industry, or general appearance.

Although Jerusalem under the Ottoman Turks continued to be regarded as a mere backward, provincial town, it did have a measure of usefulness due to its attraction as a holy city for Judaism, Christianity, and Islam. But even as a holy city, Jerusalem was not treated as a city of vital concern. The Greek Orthodox Patriarch exercised his authority from Constantinople, and the Latin Patriarchate in Jerusalem altogether ceased to exist. The Turks were aware of Jerusalem's prestige and they exploited this fact by tolerating the Jews and Christians in order to benefit from the continuous streams of pilgrims. Hence Jerusalem developed no commerce or industry. Only the annual pilgrimages provided a market for beads and similar trinkets, and these alone were manufactured in Jerusalem.

As the number of Christian pilgrims increased, the Christian sects expanded their institutions. They built additional hospices to provide board and lodging for their respective pilgrims. The number of holy places also increased, and the intersectarian jealousies and rivalries mounted correspondingly. Each Christian sect eagerly strove to acquire ownership of holy places; the Turks shrewdly played off one sect against another, and thus exacted huge bribes for every petty favor. To build or repair a church or any shrine required a government permit. This afforded the pasha an opportunity for extortion. And the pasha's appetite for bribes was voracious.

Under the Turkish system of government, all temporal and religious powers were vested in the person of the Sultan. The grand vizier corresponded to a prime minister, and the government which the grand vizier managed for the Sultan was known as the Sublime Porte. The religious communities were organized into *millets*. Each *millet* (religious body) was an autonomous body with jurisdiction over its devotees in all matters of religion and personal status, involving marriage, divorce, inheritance, and related matters. Each millet was governed by its own religious head. Thus the Patriarch of the Greek Orthodox, as religious head of his millet, was also the administrative head, responsible for the collection of taxes from his own community.

Among the Christian communities the Greek Orthodox millet occupied the highest rank. The community was headed by the Greek Orthodox Patriarch, assisted in his task by a Synod chosen from the members of the Brotherhood of the Holy Sepulchre, which consisted almost exclusively of monks of Greek extraction. This caused much resentment among the local Orthodox Arabs, who constituted the bulk of the Church's adherents.

When the Latins were expelled from Jerusalem after the fall of the Crusaders, the Western clergy was permitted to remain. So were Western pilgrims permitted to come during certain times of the year and only for limited periods. But the Latins soon began to return, and the Franciscans began to press for the aquisition of holy places. With the help of the trading republics, especially that of Venice, they succeeded in regaining several key holy places. When the trading republics declined, France became the official protector of the Latins in the Holy Land. Whenever the Franciscans felt that their rights were infringed upon, they turned to France and France intervened on their behalf.

Of all the religious groups, the Jews suffered most. While the Christians had protectors in the European powers who occasionally spoke out on their behalf, the Jews had nobody to shield them against the corrupt officials. The Jewish quarter was therefore the most neglected and most disease-ridden part of the city. It was overcrowded and exposed more to extortion than the rest of the city. Poverty, disease, and humiliation were the perpetual lot of the Jewish inhabitants of Jerusalem. Yet the Jewish population gradually increased and finally outnumbered the Christians and Moslems combined.

The Ottoman period started out most favorably for the Jewish community. At the end of the fifteenth century, the Jews had been expelled from Spain and the exiles, who were in search of homes, were welcomed by the Turks.

Some Jews settled in Safed, Tiberius, and Jerusalem. Thus Spanish Jewish immigrants became the core of the Jewish community of Jerusalem. They built a synagogue on a spot which was the traditional site of the academy of the talmudic sage, Rabbi Yohanan ben Zakkai, who had lived during the fall of Jerusalem in the year 70. Around this synagogue developed a complex of four synagogues, each with a congregation and a name of its own. But the complex continued to be called by the name of the first and most important of the four synagogues, the Yohanan ben Zakkai Synagogue.

With the deterioration of the city, the more enterprising elements emigrated and only the poor remained. In the year 1700, a large group of 1500 Jewish immigrants from the West, headed by Rabbi Judah He-Hasid, arrived in Jerusalem. These *Ashkenazi*, or Western Jews, acquired a plot near the old Ramban Synagogue and built a house of prayer. In 1721, the Arabs burned the synagogue with its forty scrolls of the Torah. The synagogue remained a ruin for over a century. During that period the Jews called that place the *Hurvah* (the ruin).

Another large group of Jewish immigrants, disciples of the Gaon of Vilna, arrived in Safed. Some of these group later settled in Jerusalem. They rebuilt the Hurvah in 1837, and the synagogue became the central house of prayer of the Ashkenazi Jews. The new structure with its prominent dome continued to be called the Hurvah Synagogue, though its official name was *Menahem Tsiyon* (The Comforter of Zion).

Obviously, the infidels, both Christians and Jews, suffered more than the Moslems. But the Arab population also suffered from the ubiquitous extortions. To be sure, they shared with the Turks a contempt for the infidels, but they were not exempt from the vicious fiscal system. In addition, the local population suffered from another evil.

The governor was responsible for a fixed quota of recruits for the Sultan's army. These were levied on the Arab population. The well-to-do paid for their exemptions, while the poor Arabs had to serve in the army. The infidels were mercifully exempt. This balanced the burdens of Turkish rule. However, the Arabs' chief shrines, the Dome of the Rock and the Al-Aqsa Mosque, were generally maintained in good repair. This was also the case with the other Moslem holy places. But some of the madrassahs deteriorated and some actually closed.

In the sixteenth century, Turkey was a superpower. Half of Europe's population was under its jurisdiction. But, after Suleiman the Magnificent died in 1566, Turkey began its long period of deterioration, and Jerusalem settled down to centuries of stagnation. Nothing really happened in Jerusalem till the beginning of the nineteenth century. The result of this stagnation was a steady decline of the city's population, so that by the turn of the nineteenth century, the city's inhabitants numbered only 9,000.

The causes of Turkey's decline were mainly internal. But the growth of the Russian Empire and the brilliant leadership of the Austrian and Polish governments were also responsible for the Turkish decline. The sultans who succeeded Suleiman were weak and indolent. The morale of the army declined, and the feared Janissaries became unreliable. Inefficiency and corruption infected their officers, and town life was preferred to the rigors of the battlefield. And the district governors were no longer as loyal to the Sultan as they had been formerly.

The Empire did not begin to totter immediately after Suleiman's death. However, the seeds of decay were beginning to sprout. Actually, the Empire continued to expand. Arabia was absorbed in 1570, and Cyprus was added at the cost of 50,000 men. But Turkey ceased to be the terror of Europe. When Murad IV died in 1640, the last of the fighting sultans passed, and his successors were mere figureheads. The government passed into the hands of the viziers or Turkish prime ministers. Some of the viziers were men of ability, but they were not the equals of their opponents, the Austrians, the Hungarians, and the Poles.

In 1682, the Turks were stopped at the gates of Vienna. Shortly thereafter, Buda and Belgrade were retaken. By now, Turkey not only ceased to be a dangerous power, but its fate became precarious. Turkey was saved from total extinction only by the divisions among the European Powers. Russia became the chief threat to Turkey. Several wars between Russia and Turkey took place, but they were mostly indecisive. In 1783, Russia annexed the Crimea; by the Treaty of Jassy in 1792, Russia claimed to be the official protector of the Eastern Christians in Turkey, as France had been for the Western Christians.

Only in the nineteenth century, when Turkey had reached a very low state, did it really try to pull itself out of its rot. It was only then that Jerusalem awoke from its long lethargy, and its history came to life again.

Before dealing with modernity as it applied to the Turkish Empire, one event caught the attention of Christendom: the great fire in the Church of the Holy Sepulchre. The devastating fire broke out in the church on the night of Oct. 12, 1808. It started in the Armenian chapel, and soon spread throughout the Church. George Williams, in his excellent work, *The Holy City*, renders a vivid account of that disastrous fire:

> The heat was so excessive that the marble columns which surrounded the circular building, in the centre of which stood the sacred grotto, were completely pulverized. The lamps and chandeliers, with the other vessels of the Church—brass, and silver, and gold—were melted like wax; the molten lead from the immense dome which

covered the Holy Sepulchre poured down in torrents; the Chapel erected by the Crusaders on the top of the monolith was entirely consumed; half the ornamental hangings in the ante-chapel of the Angel was scorched; but the Cave itself, though deluged with a shower of lead, and buried in a mountain of fire, received not the slightest injury internally.[2]

The fire necessitated extensive rebuilding. The dome had collapsed and the edicule of the Holy Sepulchre chapel had been damaged. But at the time of the fire the European states were preoccupied with the pressing problems created by the Napoleonic wars. This presented the Greeks with the golden opportunity of obtaining from the Sublime Porte the right to rebuild the Church. According to Turkish law and tradition, this privilege gave the Greeks not only an opportunity to stamp their inscriptions about the Holy Sepulchre, but also the right to custodianship of all the holy places in this conglomerate of sacred sites. The Latins and Armenians were alarmed by the implications of this development. Their worries were relieved when the sultan amended his original permit to the effect that the rebuilding of the Church would not prejudice the rights and privileges of the other Christian denominations. The rebuilding was completed in 1810.

The plan and dimensions of the Crusader's Church were not altered, but its beauty was gone. The work was executed in great haste and with little taste. The dome of the Church had to be rebuilt a few years later to prevent its collapse. And Alphonse de Lamartine, who visited the Church in 1832, remarked that "the whole (is) in bad taste

---

2. George Williams, *The Holy City; Historical, Topographical and Antiquarian Notices of Jerusalem*, 2nd ed., Vol. 2 (London: Parker, 1849), 88–89.

and of a distorted and grotesque design."[3] Leslie Farmer, writing more than a hundred years later, says: "An unknown Greek designer was in charge, and he built the hideous marble kiosk which now stands over the Tomb."[4]

3. Alphonse Marie Louis de Lamartine, *Recollections of the East*, trans. Thomas Philipson, Vol. 1 (London: G. Virtue, 1845), 325.

4. Leslie Farmer, *We Saw the Holy City* (London: Epworth Press, 1944), 70–78.

14

Jerusalem in the Nineteenth Century

Jerusalem under the Turks had slumbered for centuries, and the European powers regarded Jerusalem as a town of little consequence. When Napoleon invaded the Holy Land, he advanced straight to Acre. Jerusalem, despite its walls and towers, had no military value or political status. In the nineteenth century, however, Jerusalem emerged from its lethargy and became a center of Great Power intrigue. Turkey soon realized Jerusalem's political value and began to use the city as a pawn in the larger political game.

For Jerusalem, the nineteenth century was a period of growth and transition—growth from a small town to a city of importance, and transition from medievalism to modernity. At the turn of the century, the population of Jerusalem was only about 9,000; at the end of the century, the population had grown to roughly 55,000.

In tracing the growth of Jerusalem during the nineteenth century, several key events stand out as crucial, because they affected the tempo and even the direction of the city's development. Three of these events stand out: (1) the keen competition among the major European powers for a foothold in Jerusalem; (2) the development of improved communications with the outside world; and (3) the birth of modern Zionism. These three factors catapulted Jerusalem from its backward place of inconsequence to a foremost position of international concern.

In Jerusalem, the nineteenth century started in 1831, when an Egyptian army under Ibrahim Pasha captured Jerusalem and stimulated an accelerated process of change. It was only then that Jerusalem began to awaken from its centuries of slumber and decay. European merchants and travelers were welcomed. A policy of tolerance toward Christians and Jews was adopted. To be sure, the Egyptians ruled despotically, but it was a government without favor. However, the European Powers, principally England, intervened on behalf of the Turks, and in 1840, the Egyptians had to evacuate the country. From then on the Great Powers began to meddle intensively in the affairs of Jerusalem, and they have continued to do so well into the twentieth century.

When the Turks resumed their rule in the Holy Land, they made an earnest attempt to restore order and to centralize power in the government institutions. This effort might have succeeded, at least partially, had it not been for three powerful factors: (1) Constantinople was in great need of money, which led to heavy taxation; (2) the old disease of corrupt officials could not be cured by passing good laws; and (3) the system of extraterritorial privileges which were granted to foreign consuls undermined the government's authority.

The intervention of the European Powers during the Egyptian invasion saved Turkey from collapse. But it also revealed Turkey's weakness. Since then Turkey came to be known as the "Sick Man of Europe," and the Great Powers began to jockey for positions in the line of inheritance. Turkey's survival now depended on the outcome of international intrigue. The Sublime Porte found it necessary to grant the European Powers and their nationals special status in Jerusalem and elsewhere in the realm. The foreign powers, in order to further entrench themselves, especially in Jerusalem, intensified their concern for the Churches, and they injected themselves as "protectors" of their respective denominations. With this backing, the sects intensified their rivalries. France, Russia, and Germany were especially aggressive in asserting their concern for their nationals and their religious institutions. They erected religious buildings and even established colonies. Prior to 1840, the religious buildings in Jerusalem, in addition to the Church of the Holy Sepulchre, were few in number. After that date, their number kept growing till the map of Jerusalem was dotted with innumerable religious structures—churches, hospices, hospitals, schools, orphanages, monasteries, seminaries, nunneries, and other religious monuments. Turkey was understandably liberal in granting permission for the establishing of new shrines and new institutions. When the imperial rivalries eventually ceased, the religious structures and institutions remained and constituted major elements of Jerusalem's complex of religious landmarks. Pilgrims and tourists regard these structures as integral and indispensable aspects of the religious sites in Jerusalem.

The intrigues of the European powers in Jerusalem were subject to a number of rules. One of these was the overriding principle of "the balance of power." This principle dominated the political manipulations, and it succeeded in keeping the "Sick Man of Europe" alive for about a century longer than was generally anticipated.

Another principle governed the explosive situation at the holy places. It was known as the *Status Quo*. In the Treaty of Paris which ended the Crimean War in 1856, the Turkish government reaffirmed the rights of the various Churches to be exactly as they had been prior to the Crimean War. This arrangement was raised to the status of a sacred doctrine, according to which no change, irrespective of its justice, was to be made in the religious possessions and privileges of the various sects and nationalities in Jerusalem.

Still another rule was based on certain treaties known as the Capitulations. These treaties gave the foreign consuls the right to protect their respective nationals and to govern them in accordance with their national law.

The Capitulations[1] were born in the year 1536, when Suleiman the Magnificent concluded a treaty with France granting the French government the right to establish commercial enterprises in Turkey. The French were granted individual and religious liberty, and their consuls in Turkey were given the power to act as the protectors of their nationals. These capitulations were to be terminated at the death of the Sultan.

In 1740, the French renegotiated the Capitulations. Since France had helped to save Turkey from dismemberment by Russia and Austria, Turkey rewarded France by extending the Capitulations in perpetuity. Since France was also the official "Protector of Christianity in the East," that is, the protector of the Roman Catholics, the Latins in Jerusalem were granted additional rights in the Holy Sepulchre and on Calvary. These rights raised the Latins to a rank that was almost equal with the Greeks. But this situation lasted only until 1751, when the Greeks once more gained the upper hand.

The Treaty of the Capitulations was a rational arrange-

---

1. The treaty was called "Capitulations" because it contained a specific number of *Capituli* or chapters. The term "Capitulations" has been defined as treaties conferring the privilege of extraterritorial jurisdiction on subjects of another state.

ment when it involved equal powers. When Suleiman the Magnificent entered into such a treaty, Turkey was at the peak of its power. The Sultan knew that he could abrogate the treaty at any time it did not serve his interests. But Turkey of the nineteenth century was an utterly helpless state. Hence the Capitulations became an instrument for the country's further disintegration. By the end of the nineteenth century nearly every European power and the United States had obtained a Treaty of Capitulation.

As a result of the Treaties of Capitulation, no foreign national could be arrested or dealt with by a Turkish government official. All foreign nationals were under the protection of their respective consuls, who had the power to fine or imprison offenders under their jurisdiction. The foreign consul was also the judge in disputes between his nationals. Whenever a national of his was involved in a court case with a Turk, the consul or his representative attended the litigation as protector of his subject. The status of the foreign consul was, in a sense, equal to that of the Turkish Pasha.

More preposterous was the postal situation. Each consul ran a postal system of his own alongside the Turkish post office. Up until the First World War, a Jerusalemite could send a letter through the Turkish, German, French, Austrian, Russian, or Italian post services. As can be seen, there was competition between some of the post offices, this despite the official opposition of the local Turkish postal authorities.

At first, the foreign consuls bypassed Jerusalem. They were located only in the coastal cities where their countries had commercial interests. When the European Powers began to maneuver for positions in Jerusalem, they began to establish consulates in the Holy City. The first consulate in Jerusalem was opened by Great Britain in 1838. In addition to being the guardian of the British nationals, the British consul also became the protector of all the Protestants. Since Russia did not extend any protection to its

Jewish nationals and was glad to be rid of them, Britain obtained Russia's consent and took the Jews under its protection. Imperial interests were no doubt involved in this action. But there was also in it an element of altruism. By taking the Russian Jews under its protection, the British presence in the Holy City was strengthened and, at the same time, a noble deed of genuine benevolence was performed. James Finn, British Consul in Jerusalem, writes in his work, *Stirring Times*:

> It was distressing to behold the timidity (of the Jews) which long ages of oppression had engendered. Many times a poor Jew would come for redress against a native, and when he had substantiated his case, and it had been brought by the Consulate before the Turkish authorities, he would, in mere terror of future possible vengeance, withdraw from the prosecution, and even deny that any harm had been done him or if that was too manifest, declared that he could not identify the criminal, or that the witnesses could not be produced. Still, even then, the bare fact that some notice had been taken had a deterrent effect upon criminals who had hitherto regarded the defenceless Jews as their special prey.[2]

Even before the establishment of the British consulate in Jerusalem, the London Society for Promoting Christianity Among the Jews was already functioning in Jerusalem and, in 1841, Britain, in cooperation with the King of Prussia, established an Anglican bishopric in Jerusalem. In 1849, Christ Church was dedicated within the Old City walls near the Jaffa Gate. Thus, for the first time, a Protestant presence in the Holy City was established, and British missionaries began to work intensively for the conversion

---

2. James Finn, *Stirring Times*, Vol. 1 (London: C. Kegan Paul, 1878), 127.

of the Jews. In 1898, the Anglican Cathedral of St. George was established by the Anglican Church. The Cathedral is a splendid structure located outside the city walls, not far from the Damascus gate. The Cathedral has engaged in the normal activities of a church, especially in the field of religious education.

Another achievement should be credited to the British, although it proved to be largely academic. Religious liberty, no less, was officially obtained in the Holy Land chiefly through the efforts of Lord Stratford de Redclife, the British ambassador in Constantinople. He induced the Turkish government to issue the Edict of Toleration or the *Hatt-i-Sherif* of 1856, according to which the persons and properties of all the Sultan's subjects, without distinction of religion or nationality, were guaranteed. But it took many years and the vigilance of the Consuls before the Edict came to be honored. The Edict of Toleration was usually vitiated by the prevailing bribery. However, its presence in the law books was a great help. If one dared defy intimidation and appealed to higher authority, he might win against the local authorities.

The second consulate to be opened in Jerusalem was that of the French in 1843. It will be remembered that, as early as 1536, King Francis I and Sultan Suleiman the Magnificent signed the first Treaty of Capitulations.[3] Among the pompous titles of honor bestowed on the French King was "Protector of Christianity." This title was merely one of the extravagant phrases of flattery that Orientals indulge in when addressing somebody. This was a personal epithet, not a national function. The French, however, saw the potential advantage from such a function and insisted that this title be included in all treaties. Thus, France became the "Protector of Western Christianity in the

---

3. See pp. 108–109.

Holy Land" and the protector of the persons and properties of the Roman Catholic churches and monasteries in the Levant. In Jerusalem, the Franciscans were the custodians of the Latin shrines and holy places, and the French were their protectors. Important services at the Church of the Holy Sepulchre would be attended by the French consul in full uniform with a large following of officials. In the Church of the Holy Sepulchre, there was a gilded chair of state reserved for him.

With the increase of European travelers and pilgrims in the Holy City, and the arrival of a Protetant Bishop in Jerusalem, and the launching of the Protestant missionary activities, Pope Pius IX decided, in 1847, to revive the Latin Patriarchate. Inasmuch as the Latin Patriarchate had been defunct for over 500 years, ever since the Crusaders were evicted from Acre, this decision was significant and dramatic. With the revival of the Latin Patriarchate some of the leading religious Orders and Congregations of the Latin Church made their appearance in Jerusalem, and they built churches, convents, hospitals, and schools. Thus, the Ecole Biblique which was established by the Dominicans did creditable biblical and archeological research. The Latin Patriarchate's success is especially marked by its winning over many Christian Orthodox Arabs to the Latin Church. These converts became the core of the Latin Catholic community. The Latin Patriarchate also won over enough proselytes from the Armenian Orthodox Church and from the Syrian Orthodox Church to justify the establishment of an Armenian Catholic vicariate and a Syrian Catholic vicariate.

The Orthodox Christians did not need a protector. They were largely Easterners and Turkish subjects. However, the keen competition for a presence in the Holy City brought the Greeks a protector. Russia claimed that the majority of the Orthodox Christians *in the world* were Russian subjects. Hence, Russia had a vital interest in protecting the rights, privileges, properties, and persons of Eastern Christianity. The "Sick Man of Europe" had little choice but to grant the Russian request. Thus, Russia became the official Protector of the Orthodox Christians in Jerusalem.

Russian interest in the Holy Land and especially in Jerusalem became evident in 1847 when a silver star was stolen from the Church of the Nativity in Bethlehem. Greeks and Latins accused each other of the deed. Russia entered the fray on the side of the Greeks. Ever since that incident, Russian involvement in the affairs of the Greeks continued to increase. Prominent Russian visitors arrived in Jerusalem, and the number of Russian pilgrims grew. Among the Russian visitors were princes, admirals, military officers, and diplomats. Even before the outbreak of the Crimean War, Russia obtained a promise that permission would be granted to build a Russian church in Jerusalem. After the peace of 1856, the Russians claimed that right.

In 1859, the Russian Grand Duke Constantine came on a pilgrimage to Jerusalem and purchased an extensive plot which had previously served as the public promenade grounds and the official government reception area. This plot was located outside the city walls northwest of the Jaffa Gate. On this prominent plot the Russians built what came to be known as the Russian Compound. They built a complex of hospices for Russian pilgrims, a hospital, and other facilities. In the center, they raised an elegant cathedral. These buildings were completed in 1864. Russia also built a convent near the Church of the Holy Sepulchre, and she built an imposing structure, the Church of St. Mary Magdalena, on the slope of the Mount of Olives, near the Garden of Gethsemane. Russia also constructed other churches and religious institutions elsewhere in the Holy Land. With Russian government encouragement, the annual pilgrimages became massive. All this was presumably for the glory of Orthodox Christianity. Some members of the

Greek Orthodox hierarchy, however, were skeptical of the Russian motives and were not happy about the spectacular expansion of Orthodox institutions under Russian stimulation and control.

A latecomer in the game of power intrigue in Jerusalem was Germany, who soon caught up with the veterans and even got ahead of them. It was after the decisive defeat of France, in 1870, that the new Germany became obsessed with a drive to expand its influence and to become a power in international affairs. This intense nationalism was destined to bring massive disaster and immense suffering to the world. Germany began vigorously to penetrate the Holy City, hoping to replace France as the Protector of the Latin holy places and to replace Great Britain as Turkey's ally and friend. The Sultan granted Germany choice parcels of land in Jerusalem, and Germany began to establish a "religious presence" in the Holy City. When Kaiser Wilhelm II ascended the throne in 1888 German building activity in Jerusalem increased rapidly. An imposing Lutheran church, the Church of the Redeemer, was erected near the Church of the Holy Sepulchre, which was taller than the holiest shrine in Christendom. This lofty church is located in the Muristan, where the headquarters of the Hospitallers had once been. Since southern Germany is largely Roman Catholic, the Kaiser built another imposing structure on Mount Zion. It was dedicated, in 1906, to the Dormition of the Blessed Virgin Mary. This Catholic shrine was placed not under the Franciscans, who for centuries had been the dedicated guardians of the Latin holy places, but under the Benedictines of Beuron, a German branch of the Order.

In 1898, the Kaiser made a pilgrimage to the Holy City. He would not enter on foot as pilgrims have done for so many generations. He had to enter in a triumphal manner, riding on a white horse. The compliant Sultan accommodated the Kaiser, and he breached the city's wall near the

Jaffa Gate to permit the Kaiser to make his pompous entry. The gap next to the Jaffa Gate has remained to this day and is now used by taxis and other vehicles as a means of entering the Old City.

The Kaiser also put up a building on the crest of the hill between Mount Scopus and the Mount of Olives in honor of his consort, Augusta Victoria. Ostensibly, this castle-like structure was to serve as a hospice for German pilgrims. But no one has been able to explain why the pilgrims needed the lofty tower that came to dominate Jerusalem and its vicinity. Nor has anyone been able to fathom the mystery of how gun emplacements would aid and comfort German pilgrims. The massive edifice of the Augusta Victoria is one of the most conspicuous landmarks in Jerusalem. It now serves as a hospital.

A Protestant group from Germany arrived in Jerusalem in 1873. The group was known as the Templers, and of course, they had no connection with the Knights Templars of the Crusader period. The nineteenth century Templers were a group of pious Christians who expected the imminent Second Coming of Jesus. They were persecuted in Germany. Hence, they left for the Holy Land, there to await the Second Coming. Some of these Templers settled in Jerusalem outside the city walls in the section which is still called the German Colony. The Templers were industrious people and had a salutary influence on Jerusalem's modernization. They established a "self-contained" community and even minted their own coinage. The end of the Templer enterprise is sad. Their children fell under Nazi influence and returned to Germany. The rest of the Templers were deported by the British to Australia during the Second World War. There they could not do much harm to the British war effort.

Another admirable Protestant group that settled in Jerusalem and had a wholesome effect on the city's population was the American Colony. It was founded in 1881 by a native of Chicago named Horatio Stafford. The aim of the founder and his associates was "to render Christian service to the needy of Jerusalem" without distinction of race or creed. This group was industrious and generous. They developed successful enterprises on a cooperative basis, and extended help to the needy impartially. They gained the confidence and respect of the various Christian communities as well as of many Jews and Moslems. The section in East Jerusalem called the American Colony is where they settled and carried on their work with great dedication. Today, nothing is left of that magnificent enterprise except a hotel by the name of the American Colony.

In the same year of 1881, when the American Colony was founded, a streamlet of Yemenite Jews began to arrive in Jerusalem. These bedraggled, barefooted, half-starved, diminutive people must have appeared to the Jews of Jerusalem not unlike the proverbial Martians. They were small in stature, probably due to the severe malnutrition endemic to the Southern Arabian peninsula. They were peaceful people, skilled craftsmen, hard-working, and kindly. But they were so unlike the familiar types of Jews that the Jews of Jerusalem at first questioned their Jewishness. These Yemenites were neither Ashkenazi (Occidental) nor Sephardi (Oriental) in their religious customs. One intriguing peculiarity was their ability to read holy books upside down. This peculiar skill the Yemenites learned from childhood when a whole group of children had to study and read from one text, sitting around it in a circle. Their stark poverty was also reflected in their strange clothes, if rags can be honored with such a name.

During the first few years, the place of the Yemenite Jews was in the balance. The Jews of Jerusalem, burdened with the huge number of their poor, were weighing whether to share their pittance with these questionable Jews. Two Christian groups came forward with assistance—the mis-

sionaries and the American Colony. Christians were unknown to the Yemenite Jews, and the missionaries were
not suspected of ulterior motives. At first, both groups
were received by the Yemenites as a God–sent blessing.
But they soon learned to distinguish between the two. They
kept the missionaries at a distance, while they gratefully
accepted the proffered help from the American Colony. To
this day, knowledgeable Yemenite Jews bless the American
Colony for their assistance during those transitional years.
The destitute Yemenite Jews were settled in the Silwan
Village, southeast of the Old City. This Yemenite colony
existed till the Arab riots of 1936 when life next to their
Arab neighbors became too hazardous. They moved to the
New City where they settled among their fellow Yemenites.
Silwan thus reverted to a purely Arab suburb of Jerusalem.

To complete the story of the entrenchment of the Great
Powers in Jerusalem, it is well to note that Prussia opened
its consulate in Jerusalem in 1843. Sardinia, too, established a consulate in 1849. Spain established a consulate in
Jerusalem in 1854, and the United States opened a consulate in 1862.

Turkey's troubles did not end with the ouster of the
Egyptian invaders who were led by Ibrahim Pasha in 1840.
Russian ambitions now began to plague the Turks. As
already noted, Russia successfully pressed its claims to
bear authority as the protector of the Greek Orthodox
Church and to assume privileged status at the holy places.
Russia also pressed for additional concessions at the
Church of the Holy Sepulchre, which Turkey was reluctant
to acknowledge. But the center of dispute shifted from
religious privileges to that of the balance of power. Thus,
the seemingly harmless dispute over the holy places was
one of the main causes of the Crimean War, which broke
out in 1853. Great Britain and France joined Turkey in a
war of containment against Russia. Jerusalem was hardly
touched by this conflict because the war was fought far

from the Middle East. The outcome of the Crimean War was a victory for the Allies. Thus, Turkey was again saved from dismemberment, and the life of the "Sick Man of Europe" was further extended.

On April 14, 1856, the Crimean War ended. On April 24, a "general illumination" was held in Jerusalem to celebrate the happy event. Houses and minarets were lighted up; bonfires, fireworks, and parades dramatized the people's joy. The siege and capture of Sevastopol were re-enacted at the Citadel. Cannon were fired from the embrasures of the wall surrounding the city, and the fire was answered from the rooftops by infantry who "rushed" the Castle and "captured" it.

One of the reasons for the grand celebration was the issuance, by the Sultan, of the above-mentioned Edict of Toleration. When the celebrations were over, the Edict was practically nullified by the traditional venality of the pashas and the intrigues of the effendis. Yet things did change. The Temple Mount area, which no Christian or Jew could enter, was now opened to all.

The Crimean War did not cure the "Sick Man of Europe." Russia was still eager to hasten the Sick Man to his grave and continued to pursue its expansionist policy in the Holy Land. The Russo–Turkish War of 1877–78 proved disastrous to the Turks. The Russians invaded not only the Balkans, but also Turkish Armenia. Britain again intervened and Russia withdrew from part of Armenia. At the Congress of Berlin in 1878, the *Status Quo* of the holy places were reaffirmed. This was the first time the expression *Status Quo* was used in an international treaty, and the expression has been repeatedly used since, as if it were a holy tenet that no one dare question, let alone alter.

The dismemberment of Turkey now began in earnest. Russia was deprived of the fruit of its victory. But there were others who were more successful. These were the Balkan States.

One of Turkey's deadliest burdens was its tremendous debt to creditors in various countries. Turkey had no industry to speak of and thus no means of paying its debts. European banks therefore took over control of Turkey's financial structure. This crippled Turkey's capacity to face effectively its rebellious subjects in the Balkans.

The Balkan nations, who had been under Turkish domination since the fifteenth century, were now restive. They felt that their turn for independence was near. The first Balkan state to rebel was Greece. The revolt began in 1821 and continued to 1829, when the Greeks finally won their independence.

At the above-mentioned Congress of Berlin in 1878, Russia was permitted to keep a part of Armenia. But the biggest blow to Turkey at that Congress was the decision to grant independence to the Balkan States of Serbia, Montenegro, Bulgaria, and Romania. Bosnia and Herzegovina were then annexed by Austria, and England acquired Cyprus. Soon after that, England also established herself in Egypt.

In 1912, the Balkan States defeated Turkey and threatened Constantinople. At the Treaty of London, Constantinople, now Istanbul, was saved for Turkey, but practically all her other European possessions were lost. Turkey became primarily a Middle Eastern state.

15

The Growth of Jerusalem

The Jewish community in Jerusalem did not figure directly in the power intrigues. What did affect them was that Great Britain took the Russian Jews in the Holy Land under its protection. This proved helpful in strengthening the British presence in Jerusalem. But the Jews did not play any role of their own in the machinations that accompanied the dismemberment of the Turkish Empire. However, the Jewish community in Jerusalem grew during the nineteenth century and became the largest ethnic and religious group in the Holy City. As the Jewish population grew, they built new institutions, such as synagogues, hospitals, and schools. The hospitals and schools were especially important as defenses in the "war" against the Protestant missionaries. The word "war" is used advisedly for the Jews saw in the missionaries their mortal enemies who sought to destroy Judaism and the Jewish people. Among the synagogues built during the nineteenth century, the most important was the Hurvah Synagogue.[1] In 1837, the Hurvah Synagogue was rebuilt, and it became the central synagogue of the Ashkenazi or Western Jews. The new structure with its prominent dome was a landmark in Jerusalem. The synagogue was destroyed by the Jordanians after they captured the Old City in the 1948–1949 war, and is once more a *Hurvah*, a "ruin."

The rapid increase of the Jewish population made for unbearable overcrowding in the Jewish Quarter of the Old City. And the Arab landlords exploited their Jewish tenants. Several families would be crowded into a small hovel, and the rents were unbearably high. Many Jews in Jerusalem were also desperately poor. They devoted themselves mainly to study and prayer and sustained themselves on the pittance doled out to them from funds collected in various parts of the world. This system of collecting money and distributing it among the poor of Jerusalem was called *Halukkah* (distribution). The miserable pittance that the poor Jews received from the *Halukkah* was supplemented by weekly collections of bread from the residents of the Jewish Quarter.

When Sir Moses Montefiore came to Jerusalem in 1855, he started several schemes for the alleviation of the plight of the Jews. The most important and most spectacular of these schemes was the building of a Jewish suburb outside the city walls. This was a daring enterprise for, prior to this venture, no one had dared to remain outside the walls during the night. Woe to the unlucky person who arrived at any of the city's gates after they had been closed for the night. He was at the mercy of the robbers who prowled freely in search of victims such as our luckless latecomer. The poor victim was usually robbed of all his belongings, including his clothes. In the morning, he would enter the

---

1. See p. 100.

city wrapped in a rag covering the essential parts of his nakedness.

It was under these conditions that Moses Montefiore conceived his daring scheme of relieving some of the overcrowding in the Jewish Quarter by building living quarters for the poorest of the Jews outside the city walls. The money for this project came from an estate of $50,000 left by an American Jew in New Orleans by the name of Judah Touro. Moses Montefiore purchased a plot to the west of the Sultan's Pool, facing the western wall of the city, and built there a row of small apartments or almshouses. There were twenty such apartments: ten apartments and a synagogue for Sephardi or Oriental Jews; and ten apartments and a synagogue for Ashkenazi or Occidental Jews. The new settlement was called *Mishkenot Sha'ananim* (Dwellings of Tranquility).[2] A wall was built around the houses for the protection of the residents.[3] The problem was how to get people to move out of their hovels into these relatively luxurious homes. He had to tempt people with cash payments to induce them to move out of the relative safety of the city walls. For a time, some of those who had moved to the new suburb returned every night to the safety of the walled city.

Moses Montefiore was also concerned with the economic condition of these poor families. He conceived the idea of erecting a windmill wherein some of the residents would find employment as millers. The windmill was constructed and is, to this day, one of the landmarks of Jerusalem. Economically, however, the mill was a failure.

---

2. For the source of this name, see Amos 6:1.

3. It was characteristic of all the settlements that were later built outside the city walls to build a solid square of houses with a single gate leading to a central court into which all the houses opened. It was here, in the courtyard, that the residents led their communal life. At night the gate was locked.

It was soon overtaken by some enterprising Greeks who imported milling machines; the antiquated windmill could not compete.

Near the end of the century, a large settlement was established near the almshouses. It was called *Yemin Moshe* (The Right Hand of Moses) in honor of Sir Moses Montefiore, whose right hand supported the weak and the poor.

This new Jewish suburb outside the city walls was a pioneering venture, which was followed by others. In 1869, a second Jewish settlement was established outside the city walls. It was named Nahalat Shivah. Its founders were seven Jewish residents of the Old City, whence the name *Nahalat Shivah* (The Estate of Seven). The suburb was located on a lonely spot near the main road to Jaffa. It is now in the center of the New City. Other suburbs were built in rapid succession, among them, *Me'ah She'arim*,[4] which was founded in 1875. This suburb later became the ultra-Orthodox quarter of the city. Out of these small beginnings grew the large, thriving New City.

A new Arab quarter also developed north of the city wall, outside the Damascus Gate. This quarter includes the American Colony that was mentioned above.

Nineteenth century Jerusalem was affected not only by the intrigues of the European powers and the inner decay and decline of the Turkish empire, but also by such prosaic factors as the building of a road. It is almost unbelievable that, as late as 1869, Jerusalem had no road to its port city of Jaffa. Pilgrims could reach Jerusalem only on horseback, on donkeyback, or on foot. The trip took two to three

---

4. The name was derived from the Torah portion that was read during the week when construction began. The verse in Genesis 26:12 reads: "And Isaac sowed in that land and reaped in the same year *Me'ah She'arim*, a hundredfold." The plan for the new suburb also provided for a hundred dwellings.

days. In the year 1869, the Suez Canal was opened with great pomp. A central figure who participated in the ceremonies was the young Emperor Francis Joseph of the Austro-Hungarian Empire. After the ceremonies, the emperor made a pilgrimage to the Holy City. So that the emperor might travel to Jerusalem in a carriage, the sultan had a road built between Jaffa and Jerusalem. This road opened Jerusalem to vehicular travel and enabled pilgrims to reach the Holy City more quickly and more comfortably. The number of pilgrims now increased from year to year.

William Makepeace Thackeray once startled his readers when he forecast, in 1845, that a day would come when "the scream of the locomotive would awaken the echoes of the Holy Land." That day arrived in 1891 when a railway, connecting Jerusalem with its port city of Jaffa, was inaugurated. Instead of spending almost two days traveling from the seaport to Jerusalem, one could now reach the Holy City in five hours. This is a long and tedious trip when compared with the contemporary forty-five minute trip by automobile. However, in its day, the five-hour trip in the slow, lumbering train was a revolutionary innovation. The number of pilgrims and other travelers to the Holy City increased greatly and the city expanded accordingly.

At about the same time as the railroad was brought to Jerusalem, a modest new institution was founded in the developing New City. Boris Schatz, a visionary who had been professor at the Sofia Academy of Arts, arrived in Jerusalem in 1905. He proposed the establishment of an arts and crafts school and a museum. Two years prior to his arrival, he had pleaded his cause at the Zionist Congress in Basle, and his scheme was approved. He was voted a modest budget which enabled him to bring a teacher from Germany, the artist Ephraim Lillian. The two launched their school in an unpretentious building near the Ethiopian Church. Seven years later the school moved to a spacious building on Shmuel Hanagid Street.

The purpose of the school was to train artisans and to develop an industry of fine arts and crafts such as silver-smithing, weaving, and ceramics. The artisans produced jewelry, ritual objects, and souvenirs.

The Bezalel Museum accumulated a fine collection of traditional Jewish art objects. The museum is now part of the Israel Museum in Jerusalem. The school survived several crises, including two World Wars, the local Arab–Jewish wars, and the great depression of the early thirties. Today the Bezalel school is an institution of higher education, authorized to grant the degree of Bachelor of Arts and housed in an imposing new structure on the campus of the Hebrew University. The school is no longer an arts and crafts school; it is a college of fine arts and design, and is earning a reputation far beyond the borders of Jerusalem.

The growth of Jerusalem during the nineteenth century can be gauged not only by the large number of new religious shrines and buildings, and by the expansion outside the city walls, but also by the population figures. In 1877, there were, in Jerusalem, 24,000 inhabitants, of whom 12,000 were Jews, 7,000 Moslems, and 5,000 Christians. In 1905, Jerusalem's population was 60,000 of whom 40,000 were Jews, 7,000 Moslems, and 13,000 Christians. The dramatic rise of the Jewish population was due, in large measure, to the rise of Jewish nationalism, known as Zionism. Because of its overriding impact on the future history and development of Jerusalem, Zionism needs separate and more extended treatment.

16

The Rise of Zionism

The Israeli national anthem, entitled *Hatikvah*, "The Hope," was composed long before there was a State of Israel and was sung at gatherings long before the Zionist dream became a reality in 1948. The burden of the anthem is that despite 2,000 years of exile from the Land of Israel and notwithstanding the interminable persecutions and numerous disabilities:

Our hope is not yet lost,
The age-old hope
To return to the land of our fathers
To the city where David dwelt.[1]

---

1. When the State of Israel was established this stanza was altered to read:

Our hope is not yet lost,
The hope of two thousand years,
To be a free people in our land,
The land of Zion and Jerusalem.

The anthem has not been judged favorably by objective literary critics. It is an awkward poem, reeking with sentimentality. However, it catches the deep attachment of the Jewish people to the land of Israel, and especially to the city of Jerusalem. The anthem reflects the indissoluble bond between the Jewish people, the Holy Land, and the Holy City of Zion.

The "age-old hope" has its roots in the conscious and incessant cultivation of the national memory, and in the suffering of the Jewish people due to its homelessness. In regard to Jewish suffering, it is well to quote Leopold Zunz's classic essay on *The Sufferings of the Jews During the Middle Ages*. The author introduces his essay with the statement:

> If there be an ascending scale of suffering, Israel has reached its highest degree. If the duration of afflications, and the patience with which they are borne ennoble, the Jews may vie with the aristocracy of any land. If a literature which owns a few classical tragedies is deemed rich, what place should be assigned to a tragedy which extends over fifteen centuries in which the poets and actors were also the heroes?[2]

More important, however, were the positive forces that gave rise to the Zionist movement. These sources were an amalgamation of religion, history, literature, and daily practices out of which the Jewish culture was fashioned. They created, in the Jewish collective mind, a beautiful vision of an idealized Jerusalem for which the Jews yearned and prayed. The Jerusalem of the Jewish collective memory was a city of beauty, justice, and holiness. Obviously the

---

2. Leopold Zunz, *The Sufferings of the Jews During the Middle Ages*, trans. Rev. Dr. A. Löwy (New York: Bloch Publishing Co., 1907), 19.

people of Jerusalem were normal human beings with the
usual virtues and vices. There were among them saints
and sinners, heroes and cowards, altruists and scoundrels,
wise and simple, learned and ignorant. But the Jews who
were scattered in wide and endless exile saw Jerusalem
from a great distance, and what they saw was glorious.
Jerusalem had assumed a halo of perfection. The Jerusa-
lemites were wise and learned, pious and righteous. Even
the children of Jerusalem were famous for their extraordinary wisdom. To be sure, both the Bible and the Talmud
contain some negative testimony, which is probably closer
to the truth. But the Jew chose to believe the legendary
tales. So the Jews believed that Jerusalem was the most
beautiful, the most virtuous of cities; Jerusalem was full of
synagogues and houses of study; the Holy City overflowed
with wise men and sages. When the Jew thought of
Jerusalem, his heart was filled with longing, and he continually prayed for the day of redemption from the exile
and return to Jerusalem.

When the leaders of the modern Zionist movement
turned to the Jewish people, both in the Eastern European
ghettoes and in the enlightened Western cities, their appeal
was powered by the religious yearnings of the people for
the Holy Land and the Holy City. This notwithstanding the
secular nature of Zionism and most of its leaders. The
religious bond was forged during the millenia of praying
and yearning. And, in 1967, when the Israeli army entered
the Old City and reached the Wailing Wall, tears flowed
from the eyes of the so-called secularists no less than the
eyes of the religious. Jewish nationalist and religious
attachments have always been merged into one entity.

Throughout the centuries, Jerusalem has been the center
and goal of the Jewish popular piety and their messianic
hope. Jerusalem was at the core of the synagogue liturgy,
both in its literary formulation and in its symbolic rituals.

In every service, morning, noon, and night, the Jew prayed for Jerusalem:

> And to Jerusalem, thy city, return in mercy, and dwell therein as thou hast spoken; rebuild it soon in our days as an everlasting building, and speedily set up therein the throne of David.[3]

Especially fervent were the prayers for Jerusalem on the Ninth of Av, the anniversary of the fall of Jerusalem and the destruction of the Temple. On that day, Jews throughout the world fasted and, in the synagogues, they sat on the floor and read the Book of Lamentations and other dirges with tears running down their cheeks.

It is difficult for a non-Jew, or for that matter a modern Jew who has become distanced from his heritage, to fathom the powerful attachment of the Jewish people to the land of Israel and especially to Jerusalem. In the past this attachment expressed itself not only in the liturgy, but also in a fervent hope that God would, in His time, send the Redeemer to liberate His people from their exile, and that He would gather them to the Holy Land. For the Jew the fulfillment of this Messianic hope was a certainty. Only the timing was unknown.

In the nineteenth century, Jewish nationalism as an active movement of self-liberation struck deep roots among the Jews. It was bolstered by the rising nationalism among some of the subjugated peoples in Europe, and it was nourished by the prevailing anti-Semitism as dramatized by the Dreyfus Case. It was especially strong among the Russian Jews whose poverty and suffering had seemingly reached their climax. Added to these important factors

---

3. Hertz, *Op. Cit.* 145, 283. The fourteenth of *The Eighteen Benedictions* or *Amidah*, recited in the Morning, Afternoon, and Evening Services.

were the Russian government-inspired pogroms of the 1880s.[4]

The intense and widespread Zionist convictions, especially among the East European Jews, found their expression in the inspiring leadership of a Viennese Jew, a journalist by profession, Theodor Herzl. His conversion to the Zionist cause occurred in 1894 at the trial of Captain Alfred Dreyfus. He attended the trial as a correspondent for the Viennese newspaper, the *Neue Freie Presse*. Captain Dreyfus was accused of treason to France and was found guilty by a Military Court. He was sentenced to life imprisonment in the French penal colony on Devil's Island. Later his innocence was established. He was freed from prison and reinstated in his army post. The Dreyfus trial aroused passions not only in France but all over the world. It came to be known as the Dreyfus Affair. But the deepest passions aroused were among the Jews who saw the rapid rise of modern anti-Semitism. The Jewish people were on trial and were initially found guilty of treason. It was at that trial that Theodor Herzl decided to embrace the cause of Zionism and to dedicate his life to its advancement.

In a monograph, "The Jewish State," he outlined his dream in practical terms. While some Western Jews were outraged by the very idea of a Jewish state, the mass of the Jewish people received Herzl's statement with great enthusiasm. It intensified the hope that was in the hearts of Jews everywhere, expecially the East European Jews.

Theodor Herzl called together what came to be known as the First Zionist Congress in Basle in the summer of 1897. Almost 200 delegates from all over the world responded. There was considerable opposition by some West European Jewish leaders. However, the Congress met and its

---

4. For a vivid account of the Russian pogroms see *The Jewish Chronicle*, London, November 17, 1905.

deliberations proved to be of historic importance. At that Congress, Zionism was defined and the definition came to be known as the Basle Program. It states that "Zionism aims to create a publicly secured and legally assured home for the Jewish people in Palestine." A World Zionist Organization was founded, and a Zionist was defined as one who subscribed to the Basle Program and paid the token annual membership fee of a "shekel" (approximately half a dollar). An official flag was even adopted, a white area with two horizontal blue stripes and the six-pointed star of David in the center. This flag is now the official flag of the State of Israel.

Herzl worked indefatigably. He pleaded the cause of Zionism with the leaders of Jewish communities and with a number of sovereigns, among them the Kaiser of Germany, the Sultan of Turkey, the Czar of Russia, the King of Italy, and the Pope. At the turn of the century, Great Britain offered the Jews an opportunity to establish their sought-after "home" in Uganda. This proposal was brought to the Sixth Zionist Congress which met in Basle in August, 1903. It was a very tempting opportunity, especially since it came right after the notorious Kishinev Pogrom. Everyone felt the urgency, and some felt that the Uganda offer was a godsend. Not so the Russian delegates. There was a stormy debate. Feelings ran high. The World Zionist Organization almost broke up over this crucial issue. The Russian delegates took their stand unalterably for the Land of Israel. No substitute would do, irrespective of the urgency. The Uganda Plan was abandoned. In less than a year, Theodor Herzl died. It was said that he died from exhaustion. But the foundations he laid held firm.

When Theodor Herzl died on July 3, 1904, he was mourned throughout the Jewish diaspora. There were many who feared that the Jewish national movement that Herzl inspired, organized, and headed would disintegrate. But Zionism was too deeply rooted in the hearts and inspirations of the Jewish people to perish together with its leader, however illustrious his personality. Younger men succeeded Herzl and some proved themselves to be worthy successors. Especially noteworthy were the leadership of Chaim Weizmann, during whose term of office the Balfour Declaration was issued, and that of David Ben-Gurion under whose leadership the State of Israel was established.

Zionism spread among the Jews everywhere and, in Palestine, it found expression in the establishment of numerous agricultural settlements, many of them of a cooperative nature, known as *kibbutzim*. Land was purchased in various parts of the country, and idealistic pioneers settled on the land.

Jerusalem's Jewish population grew, and the Jews of the Holy City became the preponderant majority of the city's inhabitants. In 1913, before the outbreak of the First World War, the population of Jerusalem was 72,000, of which about 16,000 were Christian, about 10,000 were Moslem, and about 46,000 were Jewish. The Jews of Jerusalem could now be classified not only in terms of their Occidental or Oriental origins, but also in terms of their Zionist or anti-Zionist views. The latter, a small minority, consisted of ultra-Orthodox Jews, who would rely exclusively on Providence to bring about the redemption of Israel. They opposed the Zionists who, instead of relying on God, chose to engage in activities aimed at creating a Jewish commonwealth in the Holy Land. Not all religious Jews regarded Zionism as rebellion against God. Indeed, the majority of the religious Jews were ardent Zionists. They saw themselves as participants in the divine drama of Israel's redemption. These Jews were known as the religious Zionists.

The Zionists vigorously opposed the *Halukkah* system, whereby charity was gathered throughout the diaspora, and distributed in weekly stipends. The Zionists encouraged productive work, especially on the land. Some Jerusalem Jews responded to the Zionist ideology and, organizing themselves into settlement groups, succeeded in establishing a number of thriving agricultural settlements. However, the hard core anti-Zionist group has survived, and to this day, there are, in Jerusalem, several thousand ultra-Orthodox Jews who regard the establishment of the State of Israel as an act of rebellion against God.

By the end of the nineteenth century, through the attachment of the majority of the Jewish people, Zionism had become a powerful force. Some Western Jews, however, opposed Zionism. They were mostly Jews who had been affected by the forces of assimilation. Their bonds with Jewish tradition had loosened. These Jews saw in Zionism a threat to their personal security as citizens of their respective Western states.

The most important organized group of anti-Zionists was the Reform branch of Judaism whose anti-Zionism was made into a religious dogma. At a conference of American Reform Jews in the year 1885, it was officially proclaimed that:

> We consider ourselves no longer a nation, but a religious community and therefore expect neither a return to Palestine . . . nor the restoration of the laws concerning the Jewish state.[5]

It should be added that this dogmatic anti-Zionism has been abandoned by the Reform movement, and Reform Jews are now among the most ardent supporters of the State of Israel. However, at the turn of the century, anti-Zionism was a firm principle of Reform Jewry. But the mainstream of the Jewish people felt and believed in the centrality of Jerusalem and the Land of Israel. They yearned:

---

5. *Pittsburg Platform*, Fifth Point, as quoted in the *Encyclopaedia Judaica* (Jerusalem: Keter Publishing House Ltd., 1971), vol. 13, p. 571.

To be a free people in our land,
The land of Zion and Jerusalem.

The Turkish government in Constantinople as well as the local government in Jerusalem were aware of the Zionist aspirations in the Holy Land. They knew that Jewish immigration to Palestine was a central component of the Jewish national program. The policy of the Turkish government on Jewish immigration to Palestine was therefore restrictive. However, it was not arbitrary. The Turkish restrictions were circumvented by some Jews who came as pilgrims and, contrary to the law, stayed on. More effective was the opposition to the Turkish restrictions by the foreign consuls who jealously guarded their extraterritorial privileges and their jurisdiction over their nationals.

It thus came about that while the Great Powers were laboriously establishing their respective "presences" in Jerusalem, and while the Churches were jockeying for their rights at the holy places, a Jewish national movement was gathering momentum. Zionism it was called, for Zion was the focus of its goal, and Jerusalem was at the center of its objectives.

17

Jerusalem Under the British Mandate

British interest in the Middle East was based on strategic and commercial considerations. The land and sea routes to India and the Far East passed through the area. Britain wanted these routes open for trade and for the defense of the empire. When the Suez Canal was opened in 1869, the Eastern Mediterranean became even more vital to British interests. To secure its position in that area, Britain acquired Cyprus from Turkey in 1878 and established a naval base there. In 1882, Britain occupied Egypt. Britain thus tightened its control of the sea route to India and the Far East. To protect the land routes, British policy upheld Turkey in order to prevent the other powers, especially Russia, from gaining a foothold in the Middle East. At the turn of the nineteenth century Germany began to maneuver for a base in the Middle East. She courted Turkish friendship and established a visible presence in Jerusalem by building a number of imposing churches and other religious institutions. The German policy of *Drang nach*

Osten was bound to result in a confrontation with Britain. When this confrontation materialized during the First World War, Turkey chose to join Germany. This endangered the British land and sea routes to the Far East. The Suez Canal, Egypt, and the Sudan were now within easy reach of the enemy. Palestine thus became a potential battle front for Britain.

For the Central Powers, the prospect of attacking Britain in so vulnerable a spot was most tempting. Jerusalem thus became an important military pivot for the Central Powers. Djemal Pasha, the Turkish general, made his headquarters in Jerusalem and exercised his power as military governor with extreme cruelty. The population suffered from hunger and disease; epidemics were frequent. Some of the inhabitants left; others died; and the population dwindled. At the outbreak of the war, Jerusalem's population was 72,000; by the end of the war, the population had shrunk to 55,000.

Although the First World War was fought mainly in Europe, it was bound to erupt in the Middle East too. Just before the battle for the Holy Land began, Britain espoused the Zionist cause. It will be remembered that in 1839 Britain took the Russian Jews in the Holy Land under its protection. James Finn, the second British consul in Jerusalem, distinguished himself by his concern with the plight of the Jews in the Holy Land. He not only extended them protection, but also helped the destitute Jews in other ways. British involvement in Jewish affairs was also demonstrated at the beginning of the twentieth century when it offered Uganda to the World Zionist Organization.[1] It is not surprising that now, again, Britain espoused the Zionist cause. On November 2, 1917, the British government issued a declaration of policy in regard to

---

1. See p. 132.
1. See p. 132.

Palestine. It was issued by Lord Balfour, the Foreign Secretary, in the form of a letter addressed to Lord Walter Rothschild. The Balfour Declaration, as it came to be called, stated that:

> His Majesty's Government view with favor the establishment in Palestine of a national home for the Jewish people, and will use their best endeavors to facilitate the achievement of this object . . .

Five weeks later, General Allenby captured Jerusalem from the Turks, almost without a battle. In 1922, when the League of Nations entrusted the Mandate of Palestine to Britain, the Balfour Declaration was incorporated in the official charter.

The capture of Jerusalem by General Allenby on December 8, 1917 was the end of an epoch. John Finley in his *A Pilgrim in Palestine* notes:

> There is an Arab legend which I heard often in the East, that not until the Nile flowed into Palestine would the Turk be driven from Jerusalem—a picturesque way of intimating that the Turk would stay there forever. . . . But the Nile now flows into Palestine, not metaphorically but literally. I have seen the plant at Kantara, where (under the direction of a Canadian engineer) the sweet water of the Nile is filtered and started on its journey through a twelve-inch pipe across the desert toward Gaza. . . . And the Turk has been driven from Jerusalem by the same forces that cause the water of the Nile to flow into Palestine.[2]

As it happened, the liberation of Jerusalem from the Turks took place during the Jewish Feast of Hanukkah

---

2. John Finley, *A Pilgrim in Palestine* (New York: Charles Scribner's Sons, 1919), 15–16.

which celebrates the deliverance of Jerusalem by the Maccabees from the Syrian Greeks about 2100 years ago. On December 11, 1917, General Allenby made his official entry into Jerusalem. Among the select group of officers who walked with Allenby into Jerusalem through the Jaffa Gate was T. E. Lawrence of *The Seven Pillars of Wisdom* fame. Lawrence was fitted out in the uniform of a major, various parts of which had been borrowed from different officers. Allenby was flanked by French and Italian commanders of token units whose presence in the ranks of the victorious British army was due to political rather than military considerations. The Turkish army had been thoroughly defeated, and the city was taken without the loss of a single life or the slightest damage to any building within the city walls. Thus ended 400 years of Turkish rule in Jerusalem.

Unlike the arrogant entry of Kaiser Wilhelm for whom the city wall was breached in 1898 to allow him to enter on horseback as a conqueror, which he was not, General Allenby entered the city on foot, without flags or music, as a pilgrim rather than a conqueror. He proceeded to the steps of the Citadel and read a declaration in which he promised the inhabitants the protection of the British Empire and an administration based on law and justice. He also affirmed the principle of the *Status Quo* in regard to the holy places.

Jerusalem was placed under a military administration with Sir Ronald Storrs at the head. The military governor soon discovered that the most pressing problems centered around the water supply and the scarcity of food. There was enough water for the population but not enough for both the inhabitants and the army. As to food, the army was well supplied, but the civilians were left with little after the Turkish and German armies had requisitioned everything that could nourish their retreating soldiers. After cleaning up the accumulated filth and wreckage that was left by the Turks, Sir Ronald Storrs turned his attention to the water and food supply of the city.

Sir Ronald Storrs had been with the British administration in Cairo and was, therefore, an experienced colonial executive. He saw in his post as governor of the Holy City an opportunity to preserve Jerusalem's oriental features and its historic and religious monuments. He truly loved Jerusalem. At a later time, he was appointed governor of Cyprus, a serious promotion. His reaction was: "For me Jerusalem stood and stands alone among the cities of the world. There are many positions of greater authority and renown within and without the British Empire, but in a sense I cannot explain there is no promotion after Jerusalem."[3]

He disliked the Zionists. To him there was a distinction between the Zionists and the Jews. Since practically all the Jews, with the exception of a few of the ultra-Orthodox, were Zionists, one can hardly blame the Jews for regarding him as an anti-Semite. He vigorously denied that. Nonetheless, many Jews held him, in large measure, responsible for the bloody outbreaks which started in 1920 and ended with the Arab–Jewish war of 1948–1949.

Like most of the British colonial administrators in Palestine, Ronald Storrs liked the Arabs. They were the traditional natives with whom he could live. It turned out that these "natives" were also nationalists, and instead of gaining their gratitude for his "evenhandedness," he lived to see the Arabs openly rebel against the British government.

The immediate events that led to the hostilities between the Arabs and the Jews began with the Balfour Declaration. When the First World War officially ended, the

---

3. Storrs, Sir Ronald, *The Memoirs of Sir Ronald Storrs* (New York, G. P. Putnam's Sons, 1937), 465.

military administration in Palestine was terminated, and on July 1, 1920, a civil administration was instituted. Two years later, on July 25, 1922, the Mandate for Palestine was officially approved by the League of Nations. Thus, the British mandatory government was officially launched, and Jerusalem became the capital of the Holy Land.

The concept of the Mandate was new in international law. It was in truth a revolutionary idea. In place of the old colonial practice of conquest and annexation, there was this new idealistic concept which took into account the aspirations of small nationalities. This idealistic aspect of the Mandate was largely nullified by the British government when it placed the administration of Palestine under the Colonial Office. To be sure, Britain claimed that this decision was best for the country, for the Colonial Office had the necessary experience in administering territories. However, this presumably practical approach led to regrettable consequences.

Two disastrous situations soon became evident. One was the opposition of Arab nationalist elements to the incipient "national home for the Jewish people," and the other was the anti-Zionist sentiments of the colonial functionaries in the administration of Palestine. While the Arab opposition to the government's declared policy can be grasped, the opposition of the colonial officials to their own government's declared objectives is not as understandable. Why should the colonial functionaries deliberately prejudice their government's policy? But some of them felt that they were serving the best interests of the Empire by undermining the Balfour Declaration. Why, they reasoned, should Palestine become a "national home for the Jewish people"? The British fought and bled for the conquest of the land. It should, therefore, become an integral part of the Empire. The Arabs, they reasoned, were "natives" whom they knew how to rule, as the British had been ruling the natives in their vast empire. But the Jews are imbued with Western nationalism. They are therefore a threat to the imperial interests of Great Britain. This trend of thought was never officially expounded by any responsible British administrator of the land. But it was implicit in many of their actions, so much so that, during several bloody outbreaks, one of the most effective slogans among the Arabs was "The government is with us."

The brilliant general Charles Orde Wingate, then a captain, states in a private and confidential letter to the King, dated January 1, 1937:

> The administration of Palestine and Transjordan is, to a man, anti-Jew and pro-Arab. This is largely due to the fact that we seem to send only the worst type of British official to Palestine. They hate the Jew and like the Arab who, although he shoots at them, toadies to them and takes care to flatter their sense of importance. The truth of the matter is, Sir, that the whole tribe of officials out here are third rate. I don't think you will get many whose opinion you can value to contradict that statement. The contrast between the civil service here and the Sudan is startling. Hardly any of the D.C.'s here know Arabic (or Arabs) let alone Hebrew (and Jews).[4]

The response of the Colonial Office to these criticisms was not to upgrade its staff or alter its policy but rather to silence the troublemaker. He was transferred out of Palestine with an endorsement in his passport stating that "the bearer . . . should not be allowed to enter Palestine." This kind of attitude, unfortunately, typified the British administration in Palestine from its beginning to its very end.

The first High Commissioner for Palestine was Sir Herbert Samuel, an experienced British statesman, and a

---

4. Christopher Sykes, *Orde Wingate* (London: Wm. Collins, 1959), 122–123.

respected member of the British Jewish community. The Jews saw in the High Commissioner a modern Nehemiah come to reestablish the new "national home for the Jewish people in Palestine." Great hope was awakened in the hearts of Jews everywhere. Arab nationalists, however, saw, in the appointment of a Jew as High Commissioner, a serious blow to their aspirations. But the Jews were soon disillusioned. The High Commissioner was not a Nehemiah. He was strictly a British official who tried to appease the extreme Arab nationalists. Thus, despite the fact that the Jews were the preponderant majority of Jerusalem's population, he appointed an Arab as mayor. He was following, said he, tradition. Then he appointed the notorious Hajj Amin al-Husseini as Grand Mufti of Jerusalem. The appointment of this extreme Arab nationalist was an act of appeasement for which both the Jews and the British paid in blood.[5]

For the Holy City, the arrival of the British was a blessing. The city began to develop as a modern city and as a center of world tourism. However, Jerusalem remained basically a consumer society, living on pilgrim or tourist trade and on the philanthropy of the pious abroad. The responsibility for this lack of development of industry was, in large measure, due to the administrations' romantic policy. The British government saw Jerusalem primarily as a holy city which was to be preserved as a living "museum." Hence, no industrial areas were set up, nor were any other inducements offered for the establishment of industrial enterprises. This aspect of Jerusalem's development had to wait for the next phase when Jerusalem became the capital of the State of Israel. The British did, however, build asphalt roads from Jerusalem to other parts of the country. This was an urgent necessity because the roads were in an

---

5. See p. 155.

appalling state of disrepair. Jerusalem now also had a small airfield, north of the city, at Kalandia.

If, in the political arena, Sir Ronald Storrs was a controversial personality, he was a blessing to the city insofar as its religious and historic shrines and monuments were concerned. As military governor, he issued several administrative orders which have contributed greatly to the preservation of Jerusalem's monuments and to the city's unique charm. One of these administrative orders provided that:

> No person shall demolish, erect, alter, or repair the structure of any building in the city of Jerusalem or its environs. . . . until he has obtained a written permit from the Military Governor.[6]

Another edict forbade the use of stucco and corrugated iron within the city walls. This assured the strict preservation of the "tradition of stone vaulting, the heritage in Jerusalem of an immemorial and hallowed past."[7]

Still another order provided that "no building was to be placed so as to appear on the skyline of the Mount of Olives". . . . and "no building was to be of greater height than eleven meters above ground level." The general principle laid down was that the environs of the city "should be in harmony and in scale with the Old City." All building east of the Old City, especially on the Mount of Olives and in the "antiquity zone" south of the city, embracing the ancient City of David and the part of Mount Zion which is outside the city wall, was restricted. Regretfully, after 1948 this restriction was abandoned by the Jordanian government, which permitted private building in the "antiquity

---

6. Ronald Storrs, "Preface" to *Jerusalem 1918–1920* by C. R. Ashbee (London: H. M. Stationary Office, 1921), p. v.

7. *Ibid.*

zone." Jordan also built a large hotel on the crest of the Mount of Olives. In doing so, the Jordanian government marred the beautiful skyline of the sacred hill and desecrated the graves of the ancient Jewish cemetery on the Mount of Olives. The Israeli government, too, was lax in its supervision of the extensive building programs that were launched after the State came into existence. Before the public realized what was happening to their beloved city, a number of tall buildings marred the city's skyline. The population greeted the change with anger and loudly protested. The government responded to the public protest, but much harm had already been done. The tension in regard to the future development of the city persists to this day.

During Sir Ronald Storrs' administration, a city plan was drawn up. One of the seemingly minor provisions of the 1918 plan has been enforced by both the British and Israeli governments, and it has had a marked effect on the structural character of the city. The plan provided that all construction of buildings be in stone. When it became the practice to build houses with reinforced concrete in order to withstand earthquakes, the concrete walls were faced with local stone.

In 1919, a scheme for the development of Jerusalem was drawn up by Sir Patrick Geddes. It provided for a "green belt" around the Old City in order to isolate it from the New City. It also provided for the location of the proposed Hebrew University on Mount Scopus. The Jerusalem municipality has adopted these proposals as its own and has, over the years, continued to implement and expand upon them.

The most important of the Governor's achievements was the organization of a public body known as the Pro-Jerusalem Society. He felt that, notwithstanding the feuds between the various religious sects and nationalities, there was one overriding interest that they all had in common:

namely, they all loved and revered Jerusalem. He felt that they could unite for the preservation and restoration of the city's beauty and sanctity. He was confident that the leaders of the diverse communities would put aside their discordant views and bitter animosities and sit around one table to plan and act in the spirit of their common love of Jerusalem. He was not mistaken. This body, which embraced the leadership of all the inhabitants of Jerusalem, functioned harmoniously under the dedicated leadership of its founder, and its achievements were most praiseworthy. The purpose of the society, according to its charter, was "the preservation and advancement of the interests of Jerusalem and its inhabitants."

Sir Ronald Storrs brought the eminent architect and expert in urban planning and development, Mr. C. R. Ashbee, from Egypt to study the state of the neglected, half-ruined city and to prepare a report on the possibilities of constructive action toward the restoration and beautification of Jerusalem. Mr. Ashbee prepared his report and, more important, he agreed to remain in Jerusalem as civic advisor and secretary to the Pro-Jerusalem Society.

Sir Ronald Storrs also started the practice of soliciting funds from private people both inside and outside Palestine to finance the projects and activities of the Pro-Jerusalem Society. These solicitations have helped in the restoration of a number of Jerusalem's monuments.[8]

This loving concern for the city's antiquities and sanctities, for its ancient and medieval monuments, and for its inimitable charm resulted in the preservation of much that might have been destroyed by now, and in the restoration of a considerable number of the city's monuments. One of the Society's achievements is the cleaning and repair of the

---

8. This precedent was followed by Mayor Teddy Kollek, who succeeded in obtaining large sums for the restoration and beautification of Jerusalem.

Citadel, which had been used by the Turkish government as a military barracks. Another task accomplished was the cleaning of the ramparts and the restoration of the old sentinels' walk around the walls. The city's gates, too, were cleaned. Some of the gates were not only encumbered by a vast accumulation of dirt, but were appropriated by private people who had attached shops and even dwellings to the walls. Also of importance was the removal of the hideous clock tower at the Jaffa Gate. Another achievement that added to the city's esthetic quality was the naming of the Old City's streets in the three official languages—Arabic, Hebrew, and English. Plaques in glazed tiles, similar to those at the Dome of the Rock, were manufactured and placed at the various street corners. In the New City, the Society regulated the anarchic practice of placarding every wall in the city with advertisements. Notice boards were constructed for reasonably-sized notices. These notice boards are still the rule in Jerusalem.

Most important was the appointment of a Town Planning Commission which produced a draft known as the 1922 Scheme. In this Scheme, Mount Zion and the Kidron Valley were treated as part of the Old City, and the Mount of Olives was included in the proposed "green belt" around the Old City. In the New City and other areas outside the walls, the Scheme provided for residential, shopping, and industrial areas. Details were left for future planning. This 1922 Scheme had a great impact on the city's development and on future plans, of which there were many.[9]

The several town planning schemes could not be implemented during the British Mandate because of serious tensions arising from the Arab–Jewish conflict, and then, from the conflict of both the Arabs and the Jews with the

---

9. See C.R. Ashbee, *Jerusalem 1918–1920* (London: H.M. Stationary Office, 1921) and Henry Kendall, *Jerusalem, the City Plan* (London: H.M. Stationary Office, 1948).

British. However, as stated above, some progress was made despite the incessant hostilities and strife that characterized the Mandate period. General Sir Alan Gordon Cunningham, the last High Commissioner for Palestine, wrote in his preface to *Jerusalem, the City Plan*, a parting tribute to the work of the Pro-Jerusalem Society:

> I write these lines under the shadow of the British withdrawal from Palestine and therefore welcome the opportunity given me to remark on one feature of administration here which has been persistently pursued, without regard to politics or schism, by the selfless devotion of individuals of all races and creeds.

> The City of Jerusalem, precious as an emblem of several faiths, a site of spiritual beauty lovingly preserved over the ages by many men's hands, has been in our care as a sacred trust for 30 years. In these pages will be found an important part of the story of the discharge of that trust, of the efforts made to conserve the old while adding the new in keeping with it, of the process of marrying modern progress with treasured antiquity. Let old Jerusalem stand firm, and new Jerusalem grow in grace! To this fervent prayer I add the hope that the accomplishments and labors of the years covered in this book may be considered worthy to act as an inspiration and an example to the future generations in whose care our Holy City must rest.[10]

Under the British Mandatory Government, the religious communities prospered. The *Status Quo* was strictly enforced, and the government ruled by principles of law and justice. The Anglican Church, too, prospered. Its ranks were increased by British civil servants and military personnel, and by proselytes who were attracted from the

---

10. Alan Gordon Cunningham, "Preface" in *Jerusalem, the City Plan*, by Henry Kendall (London: H.M. Stationary Office, 1948), p. v.

Eastern churches. New Protestant churches also came into existence. The Church of Scotland built its St. Andrews Church in 1931, and Protestant missionary societies intensified their activities.

The only religious group that came upon evil days during this postwar period was the Orthodox Church. The Russian Revolution of 1917 stopped all pilgrimages from that vast Orthodox state. All income from the Russian pilgrims and from overseas gifts had ceased. The Russian churches, monasteries, and hospices began to decline. Their activities practically ground to a halt. The mandatory government helped the Greek Patriarchate to weather this difficult period, but the power and prestige of the Greek Orthodox Church has not fully been restored.

The Latins, however, resumed their normal tasks immediately after the war. They expanded their educational and missionary activities. The Franciscans built the Church of the Visitation in Ein Kerem and the Church of Agony near the Garden of Gethsemane. The Jesuits established a branch of the Pontifical Bible Institute of Rome.

A number of other important institutions had their beginning during this postwar period. Among these, the most important was the Hebrew University on Mount Scopus. The cornerstone was laid even before the war had ended, on July 24, 1918. The ceremony was regarded by many as a symbol of the realization of the Zionist dream. Seven years later, on April 1, 1925, the university was officially inaugurated by Lord Balfour in an impressive ceremony in the Mount Scopus amphitheater. In attendance was a large audience of local and foreign dignitaries, representing academic institutions and governments. It was indeed a day to remember.

The university started out as a graduate institution with only three research departments—chemistry, microbiology, and Jewish Studies. With this modest beginning, the Hebrew University started its distinguished career as the finest university in the Middle East. By 1947, just before the termination of the British Mandate, the Hebrew University of Jerusalem contained faculties in the humanities and sciences, a department of education, a school of agriculture, a premedical faculty, and a library of over 40,000 volumes. The faculty numbered over two hundred, and the student body over one thousand. But this was still only the beginning of the university's development. Its real growth took place in the next stage of Jerusalem's history.

On October 17, 1934, another important institution was founded on Mount Scopus. On that day, the cornerstone of the famous Hadassah Hospital was laid. Five years later, on May 9, 1939, the hospital was opened with a staff of world-famous physicians who had fled from Nazi Germany. The hospital served the population of Jerusalem, both Jews and Arabs, including King Abdullah of Transjordan, the grandfather of the present King Hussein.

Still another institution that graced Jerusalem's religious, cultural, and social life was the new YMCA. The elegant structure was inaugurated by Lord Allenby in 1933. It was the gift of an American, Mr. James Jarvis of Montclair, New Jersey. The YMCA became one of the showplaces of Jerusalem. It was equipped with classrooms, music rooms, library, tea room, gymnasium, swimming pool, and a football field. Its tower became a landmark and its observation gallery provided a grand view of all Jerusalem and its environs. Regretfully, this splendid institution later became a center of Arab nationalism, and Jews were rarely seen there. That was during the chaotic period before the British withdrawal from Palestine. The situation changed after the Jewish–Arab war of 1948–1949. The YMCA was on the Israeli side of the border, and served only a Jewish clientele. Both situations were regrettable, for the YMCA's purpose had been to serve *all* the inhabitants of the city, and to help create a harmonious society in the Holy City.

Across the street from the YMCA there is a hotel, which

has been regarded by many as more than just a commercial enterprise. The King David Hotel was opened in 1929 and has been seen by many as an institution. It therefore deserves to be mentioned. It is located west of the Old City, overlooking the Valley of Hinnom and the Citadel, thus commanding an enchanting view. It was not only the first Jerusalem hotel of international standards and reputation, but it became the host to kings and princes, diplomats and high church dignitaries, world-famous artists and writers. Its visitors' book is a veritable international "Who's Who."

One more important institution that had its beginning during the Mandate period is the renowned Rockefeller Museum of Antiquities. It is located outside the city wall, opposite Herod's Gate. The museum boasts a wealth of archeological finds from the Holy Land, and a fine archeological library. It is of interest to note that the museum is located on the site where the Crusaders encamped prior to their conquest of Jerusalem under the leadership of Godfrey of Bouillon on July 15, 1099.

The Mandatory Government started out most auspiciously. Everyone had something to gain from the new situation created by the Allied victory over the Central Powers. Britain was the knight in shining armor, come to bring salvation to all the oppressed. The Turkish system of government was replaced by an administration of justice and equity for all. The Arabs suddenly found themselves masters of their own destiny in several freed states. Palestine was divided, and the Arabs set up a state east of the Jordan. The Jews were to set up a state west of the Jordan. But this Utopia soon vanished like a dream. Did the British see their mandate as purely a messianic venture, an idealistic enterprise to relieve the burden of misgovernment and corruption and the Jewish curse of 2,000 years of homelessness? The colonial officials who administered the land surely did not. If anyone had any doubts, the appointment of Hajj Amin al-Husseini as Grand Mufti of Jerusalem should have made the situation crystal clear. Hajj Amin al-Husseini had been sentenced to ten years imprisonment for his participation in the antigovernment riots of 1920. He therefore fled the country. On May 8, 1921, he was pardoned by the High Commissioner and was appointed Grand Mufti of Jerusalem. It was the Mufti who later, in 1936, headed the anti-Jewish and anti-British uprising. When orders for his arrest were issued, he again fled. During the Second World War, he found his way to Berlin and became Hitler's advisor on how to exterminate the Jews.

The British sowed the wind by betraying their pledged aim of the Balfour Declaration, and they soon began to reap the whirlwind. In 1921, the first of a series of bloody outbreaks was started by Arab nationalists. Its avowed aim was to thwart the government's declared purpose, which was the development of a "national home for the Jewish people in Palestine." The Mandatory government feigned impartiality.

The next outbreak was more typical of the explosive situation. It occurred on the Day of Atonement, on September 26, 1925. The Jews had been conducting religious services near the Western or Wailing Wall for centuries. The Moslems owned the Temple Mount, of which the Wailing Wall is a supporting buttress erected by King Herod at the time he rebuilt the Temple. The Moslems used every opportunity to restrict and, at times, to interfere with the Jewish worship at the Wall.

The "incident" can be summarized as follows: On the eve of the Day of Atonement, an Arab complaint was made to the effect that the Jews who were praying at the Wall had changed the *Status Quo* by installing a screen in front of the Wall in order to separate the male and female worshippers. They had also set up more petrol lamps as well as a few more mats than permitted by the *Status Quo*. Also the ark containing the scrolls of the Torah was larger than it had been formerly. The British authorities confirmed these infractions of the *Status Quo* and demanded that they be rectified by the following day. On the morning of the Day of Atonement, the police arrived to check the situation and found the screen still in place and proceeded to remove it by force. The worshippers, not knowing what had transpired, were outraged and resisted. After a struggle, the police prevailed and the *Status Quo* was upheld. The indignation among the Jews was widespread and bitter. Jews throughout the world protested. The "incident" reached Parliament.[11]

In 1929, there were again serious "disturbances" in Jerusalem. *The Palestine Weekly*, in an editorial of August 9, 1929, remarked:

> It must be the irony of fate that the disturbances at the Wailing Wall should have become chronic in character only since the British took over the charge of Palestine, with the pledge to establish within its borders a Jewish Homeland, based on the historic right of the Jews to the land of their ancestors.

In the aftermath of these bloody "disturbances," "His Britannic Majesty's Secretary of State for the Colonies appointed a commission to enquire into the immediate causes that had led to that outbreak and to make recommendations as to the steps necessary to avoid a recurrence."[12] It is noteworthy that while the Jews were represented by three accredited members of the Jewish community in Palestine, the Arabs were represented, according to the

11. See "The Western or Wailing Wall in Jerusalem"—Memorandum by the Secretary of State for Colonies, presented to Parliament, November, 1928, London, p. 3.

12. *Wailing Wall Commission's Report, 1930* (London: H.M. Stationary Office, 1931), 3.

official report, by delegates from practically every Moslem country in the world, including Morocco, Algeria, Tripoli, Egypt, Syria, Transjordan, Iraq, Persia, British India, the Dutch East Indies, and others, in addition to the Arabs of Palestine. The commission held twenty-three sessions, examined fifty-two witnesses, and sixty-two documents were submitted. The commission's report is a curious and revealing document, for it does not mention the central fact that hate, spite, and venom characterized Moslem conduct at the hearings. Under the cloak of impartiality, the commission failed to mention the central fact that the Arabs were determined to bar Jewish worship at the Wall, even though the traditional Jewish place of worship was outside the Temple area.

In the violent disturbances that began in 1936, the Western or Wailing Wall ceased to be an issue. The Arabs, under the leadership of the Grand Mufti of Jerusalem, Hajj Amin al-Husseini, launched an open rebellion against the British government and a series of violent attacks against the Jews. One of the most shocking of these attacks was the murder of thirty-nine Jewish doctors and nurses who were on their way to the Hadassah Hospital on Mount Scopus. The coldblooded slaughter of medical personnel who were serving impartially all the sick of the city shocked the Jewish community more than any of the other acts of brutality perpetrated during those days. The bloody events of the years 1936–1939 resulted in a full separation of the Jewish and Arab residents into separate areas, so that the Jewish Quarter in the Old City became completely isolated from the Christian and Moslem Quarters, and there was very little contact between the Jews and Arabs of the city.

In 1939, the British government issued its inglorious White Paper, which practically repudiated the Balfour Declaration. The new policy barred, almost totally, the entry of Jewish immigrants to Palestine and forbade the acquisition of land by Jews. At the end of the war, the

British enforced the policies enunciated in the White Paper and blocked the so-called "illegal" immigrants, who were mainly the miserable remnants of the Nazi death camps, from entering the land. They were turned away with such brutality that people found it hard to believe it was Britain that had perpetrated these inhuman acts. The rigor of the antirefugee blockade led to the capture of some of the boats and the sending of the refugees to concentration camps in Cyprus or back to Germany. Some boats were sunk with their human cargoes. Ernest Bevin, Britain's Foreign Secretary, was relentless in the enforcement of the provisions of the White Paper. His pursuit of "illegal" immigrants led to stubborn resistance by all the Jews, and the extremists among them retaliated with sabotage and "executions" of British soldiers. These acts led to the imprisonment of Jewish leaders and the execution of extremists. It was a period of brutality, chaos, and bitter hostility. If the Second World War had witnessed Britain's "finest hour," the postwar blockade of Palestine's shores witnessed Britain's shabbiest hour. On May 14, 1948, the British left Palestine ingloriously. They dismantled the entire administrative organization and left. If total chaos did not follow, as the British had planned, it was because of precautions that the Jewish leadership had taken in developing a clandestine governmental system capable of taking over every government agency as it was vacated by the British. On the same day that the British left, the State of Israel was officially proclaimed.

18

Jerusalem
a Divided City

On November 29, 1947, the General Assembly of the United Nations passed a resolution which provided for the partition of Palestine into Jewish and Arab states and for the internationalization of Jerusalem and its environs. The Jews reluctantly accepted the resolution. The Arabs rejected the resolution. As soon as the British left on May 14, 1948, six Arab states invaded Palestine. Actually, the battles had raged for some time before the Mandate was officially terminated. Thus on April 12, 1948, a convoy of doctors and nurses on its way to the Hadassah Hospital on Mount Scopus was ambushed by the Arabs and seventy-eight people, mostly doctors and nurses, were murdered. Now, however, six Arab states officially entered the battle. Their aim was to undo the intent of the United Nations resolution and to "drive the Jews into the sea." And when the British left . . .

. . . the bombardment of Jerusalem (by the Jordanian Arab Legion) started at once. The British-led Arab Legion pounded the Holy City unremittingly with heavy mortars. Day and night shells hailed down on the streets, struck the improvised shelters, or exploded in homes. The shelling was wanton and savage, directed at no military objective, but striking at random through the city. . . . Within one fortnight the civilian casualties exceeded 1,000, a heavier proportion than in the fiercest times of the London blitz.

The shells were not only killing men, women and children; they were destroying the city. No shrine in Jerusalem was safe from the havoc unleashed by Glubb Pasha's[1] Arab Legion.[2]

Three times Israeli forces broke into the Old City only to withdraw. The result of the battle for Jerusalem was a stalemate.

On May 28, 1948, after stubborn resistance, the Jewish Quarter was taken by the Arabs. The young male survivors were taken prisoner, and the rest of the Jewish population, consisting of old men, women, and children, were expelled from the Old City at the point of Arab guns. The Old City thus became *Judenrein*.

The plan to internationalize Jerusalem was overtaken by the stormy events of the war. When the Armistice Agreement was signed, Jerusalem became a divided city. The Arab sector of Palestine and the Old City were annexed by King Abdullah and they became part of the Hashemite Emirate of Transjordan. On June 2, 1949, the name of the state was changed to the Hashemite Kingdom of Jordan. This regularized the annexation of the territories of Cisjordan and part of Jerusalem.

In 1947, a year before the outbreak of the war, Jerusalem

---

1. Brigadier John Glubb was the British Commander of the Arab Legion.

2. Marie Syrkin, "The Siege of Jerusalem" in *Jerusalem* ed. John M. Oesterreicher and Anne Sinai (New York: J. Day Co., 1974), 70.

was, as it had always been, one city. Its population consisted of about 100,000 Jews and about 65,000 Moslems
and Christians. The city was the country's political and
religious center, and contained many of the important
religious and cultural institutions of the three faiths. It
boasted of flourishing pilgrim and tourist enterprises and
harbored the central political institutions of both the Arabs
and the Jews. By mid 1948, that whole complex structure
had collapsed. Savage battles were raging in the city and all
institutional and commercial activities were at a standstill.
The central agencies either ceased to function or transferred their administrative offices to safer localities. The
religious functionaries were the exception. They continued
faithfully with their age-old rituals at the holy places.
Desperation and death stalked the narrow lanes of the Old
City and even more so the wider streets of the New City.

By 1949 Jerusalem was, for the first time in its history, a
divided city with a "no man's land" between the two
sectors. Where there was no land separation between the
two sectors of the city, high walls were raised. The Old City
with all its shrines and holy places and the new Arab
suburbs to the north, adjacent to the Damascus Gate, were
part of the Arab State, while the New City to the west of the
Jaffa Gate and Mount Zion south of the walled city were
part of the Jewish state. Thus Jerusalem, which the psalmist described "as a city which is firmly bound together" (Ps.
122:3), became two watertight cities separated by barbed
wire, concrete walls, and mine fields. No one from either
side could cross over into the opposite sector. It was
claimed that not even a Jewish cat could cross over to the
Old City, nor could an Arab cat gain access to the New City.
The division was total and effective. Arab soldiers manned
the western wall of the Old City, and Israeli soldiers
manned the rooftops of private houses, the Notre Dame
Hospital, and the Dormition Church. Occasionally, the
Arab soldiers saw fit to fire from the Old City wall into the

open streets of the New City causing civilian casualties. The Israeli government responded by erecting a series of concrete walls across the vulnerable streets. Thus, the two sectors of Jerusalem settled down to live in permanent confrontation and occasional bloodshed. After thirty years of British government, the Old City was again under Moslem rule, and once more it returned to the status of a provincial town, ruled from the Jordanian capital of Amman.

The proposed United Nations plan to internationalize Jerusalem died aborning. Since the Armistice Agreement between the State of Israel and the Arab States was reached through the intercession of a United Nations mediator, the division of Jerusalem presumably bore the stamp of United Nations approval. Both Israel and the Hashemite Kingdom of Jordan opposed all efforts to implement the internationalization plan. Both states based their opposition mainly on the argument that the United Nations had no moral justification to control the holy places since it did nothing to safeguard the city when it was menaced by desecration and destruction. Israel had the added argument that there were very few holy places in the Israeli sector of the city. The only important Christian and Moslem holy places in the Israeli sector of the city were the Tomb of David, the Coenaculum, the Church of the Dormition on Mount Zion, and the Monastery of the Cross. The internationalization plan applied only to the Old City and to the Mount of Olives, both of which were under Jordanian control. There was another argument against the internationalization plan. During the Mandate period, Palestine was theoretically an internationalized territory. The system collapsed because, as Britain claimed, it was "inoperative and unworkable." As to the holy places, King Abdullah argued that Jordan would safeguard the holy sites, as the Moslems had done since the days of Omar.

King Abdullah was particularly proud of his conquest and control of Old Jerusalem. His prestige among the Arabs derived from his family's former control of the holy cities of Mecca and Medina. Having lost his position as "Custodian of Mecca and Medina," he saw in Jerusalem an opportunity to restore his prestige in the Arab world. He regularly attended Friday services at the Al-Aqsa Mosque on the Temple Mount. At one of these services, on July 20, 1951, he was assassinated. His grandson, Hussein, a youth of sixteen, was with him at the time. The youth barely escaped with his life. This youth now occupies the throne of Jordan as King Hussein.

The young king consolidated his government in the capital city of Amman and has ruled the country with firmness. His consistent policy has been to concentrate in Amman not only the government but also commerce and industry. The Arab intellectual elite of Jerusalem has been drawn into Amman. Dignitaries of Jerusalem who sought positions of honor went there; some have risen in the ranks and are members of the cabinet. In general though, King Hussein has distrusted the Arabs of Jerusalem and re-garded the city as a center of hostile elements. Watchful supervision was imposed and non-Jerusalemites were usually appointed to rule the municipality. Employment opportunities for educated Arabs in Jerusalem were lim-ited; cultural life in the Old City was restricted; and the establishment of an Arab university was forbidden. King Hussein performed only one really constructive act in Jerusalem. In order to demonstrate his custodianship of the Moslem holy places, he restored the Moslem shrines in the Haram al-Sharif and regilded the dome of the so-called Mosque of Omar.

Jerusalem provided King Hussein not only with prestige, but also with badly needed foreign currency. Jordan had no natural resources or industry. It needed the foreign cur-rency that pilgrims and tourists brought into the Jordanian coffers. It is not surprising, therefore, that King Abdullah, and later King Hussein, defied the United Nations resolution calling for the internationalization of Jerusalem.

In time, the impracticality of the internationalization plan was generally recognized. It became clear that during the war of 1948–1949 the United Nations proved itself powerless. The Arab states defied the United Nations and invaded the Holy Land, and the United Nations could not deter them from their defiant action. It also came to be generally realized that the city is not a mere conglomeration of holy sites and that it cannot be dealt with as if it were only a museum of holy places. These holy places are important and must be cared for, protected, and made accessible to the faithful. But Jerusalem is, as it always has been, a city with a normal population whose inhabitants identify themselves with national, cultural, and religious institutions. The city must therefore be governed, as it has always been governed, by a civil administration of a national state. This has been the practical fate of cities, and this is the practical and logical way of governing Jerusalem.

When the General Assembly of the United Nations reaffirmed its original decision to internationalize Jerusalem, Israel reacted instantly and vigorously. On December 26, 1949, the Knesset (Israeli Parliament), which had been meeting in Tel Aviv, convened in Jerusalem and Prime Minister David Ben-Gurion declared, "We see it our duty to declare that Jewish Jerusalem is an organic and inseparable part of the State of Israel." He further declared, "Jerusalem is an inseparable part of Israel and her eternal capital. No United Nations vote can alter this historic fact." The government ministries were transferred and the Knesset has held its sessions in Jerusalem ever since.

But the European Powers refused to transfer their embassies to Jerusalem. The United States embassy, too, has remained in Tel Aviv. This despite the fact that sixteen minutes after the proclamation of the State of Israel on May 14, 1948, the de facto recognition of Israel by the United States was announced by President Truman. Not so in regard to the recognition of Israel's capital. This is still under consideration. Some nations, however, especially the Latin American and African states, did establish their diplomatic missions in Jerusalem, thus giving tacit recognition to Israel's sovereignty in its sector of the city. Those nations who retained their missions in Tel Aviv demonstrated their support of the United Nation's plan to internationalize the city. By 1967, there were twenty-one diplomatic missions in Jerusalem and thirty-three in Tel Aviv.[3]

In the Armistice Agreement, the Hashemite Kingdom pledged to permit access from the Jewish sector of Jerusalem to the Western or Wailing Wall. However, Jordan reneged on its pledge. The Israeli government chose not to resume the war because of this serious infringement on the agreed terms of the Armistice. For almost two decades after the Armistice Agreement, Jews would ascend Mount Zion where the traditional tomb of King David is located and from there gaze wistfully on their most sacred site in the Old City.

Jordan also reneged on another pledge in the Armistice Agreement. Mount Scopus, which is located east of the Old City next to the Mount of Olives, was an Israeli enclave within the territory annexed by Jordan. This enclave was of special value to the Jews because on it they had built the Hebrew University and the Hadassah Hospital. Jordan pledged to grant free access to Mount Scopus, but reneged on its pledge. Therefore, the university and hospital buildings stood empty. The only concession was permission for

---

3. For a list of foreign diplomatic missions in Jerusalem and Tel Aviv, see *Israel Government Yearbook 5727 (1966–1967)*, ed. Reuben Alcalay (Jerusalem: The Government Printing Press, 1967).

a biweekly Israeli convoy to relieve the guards who were stationed there. The Israeli government built a new university campus within the New City on Givat Ram and a new Hadassah Hospital on a hill overlooking Ein Kerem. On a hill adjacent to the new Hebrew University campus, the Israel Museum was erected and, adjacent to it, the Shrine of the Book, which houses the Dead Sea Scrolls and other precious ancient documents. On another adjacent hill, the Knesset and the government administration buildings were set up. The three hills with their respective cultural and state compounds are now a glorious sight. Israelis are truly proud of them.

Whenever the Israelis cast their eyes eastward, their hearts would sink. During the nineteen years that the Old City and its environs were under Jordanian control, the Jewish holy places were desecrated and destroyed in a vindictive and wanton manner. According to the Armistice Agreement of 1949, the Hashemite Kingdom of Jordan pledged to allow "free access to the (Jewish) holy places . . . and the use of the cemetery on the Mount of Olives." Notwithstanding these pledges, the record of the Jordanian government in regard to the Jewish holy places is shocking. Msgr. John M. Oesterreicher sums up the grim record:

> During Jordanian rule, thirty-four out of the Old City's thirty-five synagogues were dynamited. Some were turned into stables, others into chicken coops. There seemed to be no limit to the work of desecration. Many thousand tombstones were taken from the ancient cemetery on the Mount of Olives to serve as building material or paving stones. A few were even used to surface the footpath leading to a latrine in a Jordanian army camp. With the financial assistance of Pan American Airlines, Jordan built the Hotel Intercontinental—a plush hotel on the hill of Jesus' agony!

Obviously a road was needed, worthy of the triumphant showpiece. Of all the possible routes, the one chosen cut through hundreds of Jewish graves: They were torn open and the bones scattered. An Israeli collection of photographs of the mutilated graveyard bears this lament: "Because of this is our heart made sick; for these things our eyes are dimmed" (Lam. 5:17).[4]

Among the destroyed synagogues were the hallowed Hurvah Synagogue which was founded by Rabbi Judah he-Hasid in the year 1700, the impressive Nissan Bek Synagogue, and the beautiful complex of four Sephardi synagogues, generally called the Yohanan ben Zakkai Synagogue. The Hurvah and the Nissan Bek Synagogues with their prominent domes were razed to the ground; the Sephardi synagogues were reduced to empty shells and were used as stalls for donkeys.

The policy of the Hashemite Kingdom of Jordan toward the Christian holy places was of a different nature. Not that the Christians were deemed less infidel than the Jews, but the Jordanian government wanted to show that there was no need to internationalize the Holy City. They wanted to demonstrate that Jordan could be a reliable custodian, trusted to take good care of the Christian shrines and holy sites. On the whole, the Jordanians were benevolent regarding the Christian shrines. But even the Christians found it necessary, on occasion, to resist some government actions that threatened the sacred sites. Thus it was that when a Moslem was appointed "Royal Custodian of the Holy Places," the Catholic hierarchy resented this government action and resisted it forcefully. On November 23, 1949, a fire broke out in the dome of the Church of the

---

4. John M. Oesterreicher, "Jerusalem the Free," in *Jerusalem*, ed. John M. Oesterreicher and Anne Sinai (New York: J. Day Co., 1974), 251.

Holy Sepulchre and the government of Israel offered its modern fire fighting equipment. The offer was refused by the Jordanian government. The Church blazed for 24 hours till the fire was brought under control. But it was achieved without the assistance of the "enemy." In a choice between safeguarding the holy places and demonstrating its vindictive hate of Israel, the holy places could perish.

The Jordanians also removed from the Dome of the Rock the Crusader grillwork that figures so boldly in the literature of Jerusalem. To this day, the grillwork has not been located. It must be assumed that it was destroyed, an act of vandalism that was unnecessary, to say the least.

On the whole, however, Christian holy places were not molested; but neither were they assisted, as had been the case under the British Mandate and later under the Israeli government. Generally, the principle of the *Status Quo* was observed.

In 1961, the Jordanian government, acting in accord with the principle of the *Status Quo*, arbitrated between the Greek Orthodox Patriarchate, the Latin Custody of the Holy Land, and the Armenian Patriarchate, and brought about an agreement between these religious communities to cooperate in the restoration of the Church of the Holy Sepulchre. This agreement, which was achieved after years of complicated negotiations, led to the launching of an ambitious program of restoration. This joint effort was pursued with admirable cooperation and splendid results. The Church of the Holy Sepulchre began to show promising signs of becoming worthy of the shrine's sanctity in Christendom.

Regrettably, the Jordanian government abandoned the British plans and regulations aiming at the preservation of the city's monuments and the city's special character as a Holy City. New construction was not restricted in regard to location or to height of the buildings. As already mentioned,[5] a large hotel was erected by the government on the crest of the Mount of Olives. This structure mars the beautiful skyline of the sacred hill. Archeologists cannot forgive the Jordanian government, as well, for allowing private residences to be put up in what has been called the "archeological zone" south of the city wall, on the site of the ancient City of David.

Israel's declared policy in regard to religious institutions was incorporated in its Proclamation of Independence, which stated:

> The State of Israel . . . will guarantee freedom of religious conscience, education, and culture; and will safeguard the Holy Places of all religions.

In order to implement this policy, the Israeli government included in its cabinet a Ministry of Religions to assist the religious communities in their various activities without interfering in their internal affairs. The Israeli government thus demonstrated the paramount importance that it attached to its pledge to "guarantee freedom of religious conscience, education, and culture" and to "safeguard the Holy Places of all religions." The test of Israel's implementation of its official declaration came after the Six-Day War, when the Old City, with its many sacred sites and diverse religious communities, came under its control. This tale, however, will be dealt with in the next chapter.

As already intimated, the Arabs not only rejected a final peace settlement, despite the provisions of the Armistice Agreement, but they hermetically sealed the two sectors of Jerusalem. However, at the start of the Catholic Holy Year of 1950, the Israeli government proposed that pilgrims and tourists be permitted to cross freely from one sector of the city to the other. Negotiations were conducted through the

---

5. See pp. 164–165.

United Nations Armistice Commission. The outcome was a procedure which allowed free passage for tourists and pilgrims from Jordan to Israel, but not in the reverse direction. This procedure was instituted, and a permanent frontier post was established, at a point that came to be known as the Mandelbaum Gate. Local Christians, too, were permitted to enter the Old City for the celebration of Christmas. By 1952, the governments of Israel and Jordan had established a permanent liaison at the Mandelbaum Gate. Weekly meetings were held between the representatives of the governments, and they resolved problems involving the crossing of people from one sector of the city to the other. Jews and Israeli Moslems, however, were never permitted to cross into the Old City.

During the nineteen years of Jordanian rule in the Old City, the Jordanian sector of Jerusalem experienced an exodus of many of its intellectual elements to Amman and to other countries. As a result, the Arab population of Jerusalem remained almost stationary. In 1948, the Arab population, both Moslem and Christian, was about 65,000, and in 1967, it was about the same. However, the composition of the Arab population underwent a radical change. In 1948, there were 40,000 Moslems and 25,000 Christians, but in 1967, there were 54,000 Moslems and only about 11,000 Christians. The two Arab suburbs outside the Damascus Gate, known as Wadi El Joz and Sheikh Jarrah, expanded northward to Mount Scopus.

The Jordanian government's deliberate neglect of the Old City of Jerusalem in favor of Amman was resented by the Arab residents of Jerusalem. To meet this anti-Jordanian sentiment, King Hussein declared Jerusalem the "Spiritual Capital" of the kingdom. This gesture, whatever its practical meaning, came too late. It was announced in 1966, a year before the outbreak of the Six-Day War, when the Old City passed from Jordanian to Israeli control.

The Jewish sector of the city rapidly grew. There was a

large influx of immigrants consisting of the remnants of the Nazi death camps and the flood of Jewish refugees from the Arab states. The Jewish population grew during these two decades from about 100,000 to an estimated 199,000.

The economic basis of the Jewish sector of the City also changed tremendously. Hotels were erected to accommodate the rapidly increasing tourist trade, and areas were zoned to accommodate the new industries. Moving the capital to Jerusalem brought an influx of government workers and provided employment for many residents. This is equally true of the many religious and cultural institutions which made Jerusalem their home. The Hebrew University Campus in the New City became the center of culture, learning, and research. Its student enrollment reached 12,000, and its educational and research standards were recognized in academic circles as the highest in the Middle East. By 1967, the Hebrew University had a number of new faculties, among them the faculties of medicine, social sciences, dentistry, pharmacy, and law.

Since the establishment of the State of Israel, a number of new Jewish holy places have come into existence in the Jewish sector of Jerusalem, and some ancient holy places assumed new significance. On Mount Zion, there is the traditional Tomb of King David. Since access to the Western or Wailing Wall was blocked by the Jordanian government, this tomb became the holiest site available to the Jews. For nineteen years, the Tomb of David was the focus of Jewish pilgrimage.

Next to the Tomb of King David, there is the Holocaust Cellar which houses many soul-stirring remnants and mementos of the Nazi Holocaust in which 6,000,000 Jews, including over a million Jewish children, were exterminated. Ashes from the crematoria, soap made of human fat, and sacred items partially burned or otherwise desecrated by the Nazis are among the mementos exhibited.

An eternal light burns in memory of the martyrs. This Cellar has come to be regarded as one of the Jewish holy places in Jerusalem.

On one of the hills of Western Jerusalem, there is a more important memorial to the six million victims of the Holocaust—the *Yad Vashem* on Memorial Hill. This is the official memorial set up by the government. The solemn interior, with its everlasting flame which commemorates the Nazi victims, and the exhibits of the Holocaust move people to tears. Notables who come to Israel on official missions usually pay their respects to the martyrs at the Yad Vashem memorial almost as a matter of proper diplomatic etiquette. This, too, has become a holy place for the Jews.

On the neighboring hill called Mount Herzl, there is the tomb of the founder of the modern Zionist movement. In age, it can hardly compare with that of the traditional sepulchre of King David, which is 3,000 years old. However, the Jewish people have come to see Theodor Herzl as a modern "King in Israel" sent by God to help deliver His people from its suffering and exile. To be sure, there are Jews who repudiate this seemingly extravagant statement, but these people also negate the State of Israel itself. The great majority of Jews, religious and secular, regard the memory of Theodor Herzl with reverence. This tomb, too, is one of the modern Jewish holy places in Jerusalem.

On the same hill, there is a large military cemetery. There are rows upon rows of simple, yet dignified, stones commemorating soldiers of all ranks and of all Israel's wars. In this national cemetery are also buried seven Jewish parachutists whom the British dropped behind the German battle lines in World War II and who perished at the hands of the Nazis. In this cemetery, there are several common graves and memorials to groups who died at sea or on land and whose remains have never been recovered, as well as civilians who perished in the siege of Jerusalem during the War of Independence. This cemetery, too, cannot compare with the ancient cemetery on the Mount of Olives. But to the parents, wives, and children of those interred on Mount Herzl, these heroes are worthy of national reverence. And the nation concurs in this sentiment. This cemetery, too, is a modern holy place in Jerusalem.

By June 1967, Israel and Jordan exercised full sovereignty over their respective sectors of Jerusalem. Although many governments, including the European Powers and the United States, withheld official recognition of this de facto sovereignty, they did not challenge it. This division of Jerusalem into Jordanian and Israeli sectors became frozen, and a *modus vivendi* was established.

While this status quo was in force, a memorable event occurred, especially for the Catholic communities. In 1964, Pope Paul VI came to Jerusalem as a pilgrim. Most of the Christian holy places were in the Jordanian sector. However, the Pope crossed over to the Jewish sector and visited the Church of the Dormition. He was met by Israel's president and the two dignitaries exchanged cordial greetings. The Pope's pilgrimage left a deep impression on all the communities of the Holy City.

This seemingly peaceful situation did not last. It was radically altered on the morning of June 5, 1967 when the Six-Day war erupted. The Armistice Agreeement and the *modus vivendi* were ended, and a new epoch was to begin in Jerusalem's history.

19

Jerusalem Reunited

In May 1967, a powerful Egyptian army crossed the Sinai Peninsula and threated to strike at Israel's center of population. Syrian and Jordanian armies, too, were massed on Israel's frontiers. The Egyptian President, Abdul Gamal Nasser, suddenly served notice on the United Nations Emergency Force to quit the Gaza Strip and the Sinai desert. They departed. He then closed the Straits of Tiran to Israeli shipping. For three weeks, the Israeli Prime Minister, Levi Eshkol, and Foreign Minister, Abba Eban, negotiated with the maritime nations to open the Tiran Straits for Israeli shipping. Nothing was done. The outcome was the Six-Day War, in which the Israeli forces decisively defeated the armies of Egypt, Syria, and Jordan. As in previous Arab-Israel wars, the United Nations saved the defeated Arab states from total humiliation by ordering a cease fire. However, this spectacular victory resulted in the capture of the Old City of Jerusalem, Sinai, and the territories on the west bank of the Jordan River by the Israeli forces.

When the war broke out on June 5, 1967, the Israeli Prime Minister sent a message to King Hussein urging him to stay out of the war. King Hussein responded by starting a bombardment of the New City of Jerusalem. The Hadassah University Hospital in Ein Kerem was hit several times. Some sections of the city were repeatedly bombarded. Israel did not respond with a bombardment of the Old City.

The battle for Jerusalem lasted three days. The fighting was fierce. The Israeli forces approached the Old City from the north, which is the historic route of attacking armies. But instead of assaulting the Herod Gate, the Israeli army swerved eastward, rounded the northeast corner of the city wall, and stormed the Lions' or St. Stephen's Gate. The Old City was captured on June 7, on the third day of the war. When the Israeli soldiers reached the Western or the Wailing Wall, they stopped and stood in great awe. They could not believe their eyes. Many wept from joy. Even so-called secularists found themselves literally moved to tears and kissing the huge hallowed stones of the wall. Some soldiers prayed; others just stood in a state of stupor and disbelief, wondering whether it was not merely a dream. It was in truth a miracle comparable to that of the recapture of Jerusalem by the Maccabees 2,100 years before. The chief rabbinate of Israel declared that day (the 28 of Iyar in the Hebrew calendar) as a festival to be known as *Yom Yerushalaim*, the Day of Jerusalem. The day was to be observed annually by reciting the traditional *Hallel* (Ps. 113–118) during the morning service.

That day, Wednesday, June 7, 1967, was the first day in 780 years, since the city was occupied by Saladin, that the Muezzin's call to prayer was not heard in the Holy City. Two days later, on Friday of the same week, only a few lonely Moslems prayed in the Al-Aqsa Mosque. But this silence was not for long. On the following Friday, the thunder of war was already silent and all restrictions were lifted. Through the loudspeakers at the corners of the Temple Mount, the Muezzin's call to prayer once more was heard throughout Jerusalem: "Come to salvation. Allah is great. There is no god but God." And the Moslems once more gathered in their thousands on the Temple Mount for their regular Friday worship.

Mount Scopus was no longer cut off from West Jerusalem, and on Friday, June 10, 1967, the Hebrew University flag was hoisted on the roof of the University's library building on Mount Scopus, and the emblem of the Hadassah Hospital was raised on the roof of the desolate building that had been the Hadassah University Hospital. With these ceremonies, the historic link between Mount Scopus and the New City was forged again.

On June 19, the city was officially reunited, "never to be divided again." So declared the Jews. And they have been ready to defend this resolution with their blood. The government declared that the status of Jerusalem was not negotiable in any peace treaty. The whole city, declared the Knesset, is the capital of Israel. On the same day, Israel's Foreign Minister, Abba Eban, informed the United Nations' General Assembly of Jerusalem's unification. Among other points that he stressed was the following:

> Even after several Jordan bombardments and bombing sorties had taken place, with loss of Israeli life and damage to our towns and cities, we offered Jordan the opportunity to disengage. . . . At noon I sent a message to the Jordanian monarch through General Bull. The message was plain: Israel will not attack any State which refrains from attacking it. The message . . . was answered by the crash of shells falling in Jerusalem's streets and buildings. For the second time in twenty years that city, whose name stirs the

deepest historic memories, was wantonly converted by Jordan forces into a battlefield. Jordan . . . had gambled with destiny and incurred the full responsibility of unprovoked war.[1]

The United Nations condemned Israel's unilateral declaration. But the united city has remained the de facto capital of Israel, as it had been in the biblical, Hasmonean, and Herodian days.

On the same day, June 19, 1967, the barriers between the two sectors of the city, including walls, roadblocks, mine fields, and barbwire began to disappear. The populations of the two sectors immediately began to mingle. At first, it was mainly curiosity that motivated the crosscurrents of the population. Everyone wanted to explore the nineteen-year-old mystery on the other side of the sealed boundary. Before long, the situation began to stabilize; tension began to subside; and stability became the norm. Commerce revived and prosperity raised the spirits of the inhabitants. The economy of the two sectors began to be increasingly interlocked. Some joint Arab-Jewish enterprises were launched. Aided by government policy, tourism increased, and light industry was introduced. The inhabitants, both Jews and Arabs, enjoyed unprecedented prosperity, and the standard of living rose rapidly. High wages and full employment of the Arab unskilled workers raised the ordinary Arab's standard of living and partially bridged the wide gap between the upper and lower strata of the Arab population.

Despite the economic well-being of the Arab population, many Arabs have either continued to oppose Jerusalem's status as a Jewish city, or have been undecided on the

---

1. Quoted by Yehudah Blum, "The Judicial Status of Jerusalem" in *Jerusalem*, ed. John M. Oesterreicher and Anne Sinai (New York: J. Day Co., 1974), 123–124.

issue. When the Arabs of Jerusalem were offered Israeli citizenship, most of them preferred to remain Jordanian nationals. In municipal elections, a number of Arabs participated, but none would serve on the city council. Some have ascribed this Arab aloofness to intimidation by extreme Arab nationalists. Some have ascribed this Arab reluctance to genuine opposition to Israeli sovereignty in Jerusalem.

Since Jerusalem was reunited, a new era dawned on the Holy City. During the nineteen years, when the city was divided, the Jewish sector had a truncated existence. It was situated at the dead end of a narrow corridor that connected the city with the coastal plain. It was also situated on a frontier, surrounded on three sides by hostile neighbors. After unification, Jerusalem became once more the center of the country with a hinterland of its own. It was far removed from the frontiers, and the city became an important regional center.

Aided by government policy, the city expanded rapidly. Extensive new suburbs have grown up all around. The geographic division between the Jewish and Arab sections was erased. The Jewish New City was no longer exclusively west of the Old City. Jerusalem spread northward and eastward, so that the Jewish and Arab suburbs merged into a densely populated ring around the Old City, soon stretching into distant areas in all directions.[2] However, the core of the city is still within the massive sixteenth century walls of the Old City.

From the start of Israel's independence, a liberal and helpful policy was established in regard to the religious communities and institutions. After the Six-Day War, Israel reimbursed all the religious institutions for damages suf-

---

2. In mid-1976, it was officially announced that the population of Jerusalem exceeded that of Tel Aviv. Jerusalem thus became the largest city in the Holy Land.

fered during the war, even if the damages were inflicted by the Jordanian army. Israel has also granted the Anglican Church in Jerusalem the status of a recognized religious community, which had been denied them by both the Turks and the English during their respective periods of rule in Jerusalem. Freedom of worship has been conscientiously protected, and excellent relations with the various religious institutions have been established. The holy places have been guarded and the *Status Quo* maintained. The holy places were made more accessible to their devotees. Church institutions have been exempted from payment of customs duties and other taxes.

A British official, Mr. C. R. Ashbee, in his book, *A Palestine Notebook*, offered advice to the State of Israel. Said he:

> No, my Zionist friends, you want a little political philosophy. Convince the world that you are prepared to administer Palestine and its sacred places in the interests of Islam and Christendom as well as your own, and the world may give it to you![3]

Israel's experience has not substantiated these words of wisdom. The world does not give a land to a people because it has proven itself deserving. Regretfully, a land must be won. If Israel has administered Jerusalem for the benefit of all its inhabitants, and for the benefit of all its religious communities, it is not in order to receive Jerusalem from the world, but because such administration is part of its national system of ethics, which has been cultivated for thousands of years. One can quote many biblical and rabbinic sources in support of this thesis. But more important for Israel's credibility as a friendly and

---

3. C.R. Ashbee, *A Palestine Notebook, 1918–1923* (London: William Heinemann Ltd., 1923), 68.

helpful government are the statements of Christian pilgrims who have been in Jerusalem within the last few years. Thus, Rev. Joseph P. Brennan sums up today's accessibility to the holy places in Jerusalem:

> Rarely in her millenial history has Jerusalem known such stability and security as she knows today. Rarely has access to the holy places been so effortless and free of risk as it is today for members of each of the great religious traditions. Certainly Jewish pilgrims have a freedom of access that was long denied them. The number of pilgrims and tourists to Jerusalem has risen steadily in recent years, and among these have been numbered tens of thousands of citizens of the various Arab States who enter Israel each year to visit relatives and shrines (both Christian and Muslim), and who experience no harassment because of their nationality.[4]

Needless to say, the traditional policy of the *status quo* has been scrupulously observed, not because the *status quo* represents a just definition of the rights of the various religious communities, but any attempt at alteration, however just and reasonable, would open a veritable Pandora's box. The *status quo* is a sacred cow that no government dares touch.

The Israeli government has also maintained the *millet* system which it inherited from the Mandatory government. According to this Turkish institution, each recognized religious community has the legal power to administer the religious and personal status laws within its community. This includes marriage, divorce, and the administration of religious endowments. Each religious community has its own religious courts with power to adjudicate all matters

---

4. Rev. Joseph P. Brennan, "Jerusalem, a Christian Perspective," in *Jerusalem*, ed. John M. Oesterreicher and Anne Sinai (New York: J. Day Co., 1974), 229.

of religious practice and personal status. The decisions of these courts are enforced by the civil authorities. The government does not interfere in the internal affairs of the religious communities and strictly limits itself to the tasks of counselling, assisting, and protecting the various religious groups.

This harmonious situation was disturbed by an unfortunate incident. On August 21, 1969, a fire broke out in the Al-Aqsa Mosque. The fire was started by a demented tourist from Australia, Michael Rohan by name. The arsonist had declared himself king of Jerusalem, and his aim, said he, was to hasten the rebuilding of Solomon's Temple. The self-declared king of Jerusalem was sent to an insane asylum and then deported. The damage he did was doubly painful. The fire destroyed the precious and the irreplaceable pulpit which had been acclaimed as the most beautiful of its kind. This pulpit was made in 1189 by an artist in Aleppo and was brought to Jerusalem by order of Saladin. It was "a magnificent example of the finest arabesque work in wood."[5] Even more painful was the malicious use that Arab nationalist elements made of the unfortunate conflagration. They spread the rumor that the Israeli government deliberately set the sacred Al-Aqsa Mosque on fire as part of a plot to take over the Temple Mount and rebuild the Jewish Temple. The lie was too big to stick. The crisis passed and tranquillity was restored.

It is more pleasant to note that the work of restoring the Church of the Holy Sepulchre continued in complete harmony between the three major Christian communities in Jerusalem. This is a most remarkable development in interchurch relationships at the Holy Sepulchre. Considering the keen jealousies that have marred the sanctity of the

---

5. James Smith, *A Pilgrimage to Palestine* (Aberdeen: no publisher listed, 1895), 85.

holiest site in Christendom, the agreement between the sects and the extensive restoration which has at last been completed is nothing short of a miracle. Unable to agree on the contents of mosaics to decorate the restored main cupola over the tomb of Jesus, all agreed to compromise on a stunning white marble and gold leaf dome.

The restoration, it is claimed, cannot recreate the original Constantine Basilica. But it has restored many of the artistic details of the past and blended them with some modern artistic expressions to create an inspiring atmosphere for Christian worship.

The Armenian Patriarchate, which shares with the Greek Orthodox Patriarchate and with the Custody of the Holy Land (Latins) the main structure of the Church of the Holy Sepulchre, owns several chapels in the Church and the section of the Church where the quarters of their monks are located. Above this section, the Armenians have an attractive chapel. The restoration of the Armenian section of the Church of the Holy Sepulchre and the chapel above it was completed in the summer of 1975. The Armenians celebrated this event with jubilation. The Catholicos of All Armenians, Vazken I, came from Armenia to participate in the dedication of the restored Armenian section of the Church of the Holy Sepulchre. The Armenians also celebrated the official opening of a newly built seminary. This spacious building is located in the Armenian Quarter, opposite the entrance to their St. James Church.

Another event, touching on the Christian community, was the purchase by the Israel government of most of the real estate owned by the Soviet Union in Jerusalem. Israel acquired, in 1964, all of the Russian Compound except the Cathedral and a couple of other religious buildings. The hospices and the other buildings, which had not been used by Russian pilgrims since the 1917 Revolution, have been temporarily used as courts of law, police headquarters, and government offices. The Israel Supreme Court was housed here until it moved to its permanent home in the beautiful structure next to the Knesset. The ultimate use of that large area in the center of the New City has not yet been definitely determined.

Another restoration project involved the synagogues demolished by the Arabs after 1948. The complex of four Sephardi synagogues under one roof, generally called by the name of the oldest, the Yohanan ben Zakkai Synagogue, was the first to be restored. After four years of expert restoration, the four synagogues were rededicated in 1972. The floor of these synagogues is sunk about three meters below street level, as it had been originally. Arks for the Torah scrolls were brought from old synagogues in Italy and Turkey; pulpits and candelabra were gathered from various old Sephardi synagogues. The second synagogue to be restored was the 700-year-old Ramban Synagogue. The synagogue was rededicated in 1976. The Hurva Synagogue, the largest of all the synagogues of the Old City, which had been systematically dynamited by the Jordanians, is still in ruins.

Jerusalem has also experienced great growth in cultural and educational areas. No sooner was the city reunited than a vigorous building program was initiated on Mount Scopus. To facilitate this building program, it was necessary to level the narrow ridge of Mount Scopus into a plateau. On that plateau were now placed additional buildings for the Hebrew University and the expanded Hadassah Hospital. The dozens of spacious buildings of the University house the faculties of the humanities and the social sciences. The Givat Ram campus in the New City houses mainly the science faculties.

In March, 1975, the Hebrew University observed its fiftieth anniversary. Four hundred and sixty delegates from twenty-one countries were in attendance. The Israeli Minister of Education and Culture characterized the university as a "jewel in Israel's crown." Judging the university by its

achievements, despite the incessant wars and its disloca-
tion from Mount Scopus during the nineteen years of
Jordanian rule, one can readily accept the Minister's char-
acterization. At the time of this jubilee celebration, the
Hebrew University had an enrollment of 18,000 students.
The enrollment currently stands at 24,000. Since its incep-
tion, the university has granted over 93,000 Bachelors,
Masters, and Doctors degrees. The university has undoubt-
edly had a beneficial impact on the intellectual, moral, and
cultural life of the country. It has served as a mother of
universities. It nurtured Tel Aviv University during its first
years of existence, repeated this role for Haifa University,
and then again for Ben-Gurion University in Beersheba.
Members of the Hebrew University faculty commuted
between Jerusalem and the fledgling universities, filling
their still empty chairs while they were recruiting their
own faculties.

The Hebrew University has also developed a number of
cooperative study programs with universities abroad, mainly
involving student exchange projects. One of the most
striking of these programs is with the Pontifical Bible
Institute of Rome. Currently there are twenty-one Catholic
priests and postgraduate students of the Bible Institute
from sixteen countries enrolled in this joint program.

The Hadassah Hospital, too, divides its functions between the main medical center at Ein Kerem and the
restored hospital on Mount Scopus. On October 21, 1975,
the restored and expanded hospital on Mount Scopus was
dedicated. Over 2,000 Americans, mostly members of the
Hadassah Organization, came to Jerusalem to attend the
dedication ceremonies.

Jerusalem has also witnessed the expansion of many
institutes of higher Talmudic studies, too many to be
described here. These institutes or *Yeshivot* have attracted
many scholars and promising students, and the city has
been culturally enriched by them.

Both the Bezalel Art Institute and the Rubin Conservatory of Music are now housed in new and expanded quarters on the campus of the University of which they are a part.

Among the Arab inhabitants there have been revolutionary changes in the fields of education and culture. Schools have been erected and standards have risen. These changes have not impaired the ethnic diversity of the population. Every effort has been made to encourage the cultural uniqueness of each community: Moslem, Christian, and Jewish. For example, most of the Moslem schools continue to use the Jordanian curriculum. Arab periodicals, among them daily newspapers, are being published, and cultural activities are fostered in the community centers that have been established in the Old City and in the new Arab suburbs. The Arabic language is a compulsory subject in the curriculum of the Jewish schools.

The most exciting scholarly activity since the reunification of the city has been the intensive archeological research initiated in Jerusalem. It was an American, Professor Edward Robinson, who started modern archeological research in the Holy Land in the 1830s. He was followed by other scholars who were motivated by a desire to rediscover the Holy City and to gain a better understanding of the Holy Scriptures.

It should be noted that the archeologists are unearthing many significant finds relating to Jerusalem's history. They have made many advances as well in the understanding of the ancient, medieval, and premodern topography of Jerusalem. Distinguished archeologists did valuable work in Jerusalem prior to 1967. But never have archeologists labored with such intensity and enthusiasm as after the city was unified. The main excavations have taken place in the Jewish Quarter and south of the Temple Mount, extending to where the ancient city of David was located. Due to dramatic finds such as King Hezekiah's Wall, built in the last decade of the eighth century B.C.E., the true configuration of Biblical Jerusalem, a much larger city than previously imagined, has now been established.

The Jewish Quarter was always the most wretched section of the Old City. A late nineteenth century American pilgrim wrote:

> The Jews, it is said, form almost two-thirds of the popula-
> tion of the city. They occupy a section which covers the
> greater part of the eastward slope of Zion; and the Jewish
> Quarter is the most wretched in the whole wretched town.
> Its inhabitants are quiet and subdued in bearing; they make
> no claims to their hereditary rights in the Royal City of their
> kings; they simply and silently and patiently wait.[6]

But the desolation after the nineteen years of Jordanian rule was beyond description. Following the expulsion of the Jewish residents in 1948, the miserable hovels of the area were occupied by homeless Arab derelicts and refugees from other cities. They moved in with their meager possessions, including their animals. They even occupied half-destroyed hovels and burned-down synagogues. No essential repairs were made during the winter rains, and these flimsy hovels further deteriorated. When the Jews returned after the Six-Day War, they were dismayed at the sight of destruction and ruin.

The Israeli government immediately launched an intensive program to rehabilitate and repopulate the Jewish Quarter. The debris was removed, the squatters were compensated and relocated in habitable homes, and a rebuilding plan was adopted. A firm principle was established that no building was to be erected in the area without clearance from the archeologists. Every plot of

---

6. Laurence Hutton, *Literary Landmarks of Jerusalem* (New York: Harper, 1895), 19.

land was dug up by a team of archeologists before any construction was done. By now, the Jewish Quarter has been excavated and explored by the archeologists, and new houses have been installed. The new buildings blend with the style and character of the Old City. Among the many significant discoveries made by the archeologists was the location of the New Church of St. Mary, known as The Nea[7], which Justinian had erected. Some scholars used to locate this church in the southeast portion of the Temple Mount. The Church of St. Mary was uncovered near the Yohanan ben Zakkai Synagogue. The discovery of Hezekiah's Wall and its significance has already been mentioned. It has also been established that, notwithstanding the logic of the historians, there was no wall between the Temple Mount and the Upper City. The fact that it took the Roman legions an additional month to capture the Upper City after their occupation of the Temple Mount was probably due to the desperate resistance of the embattled Jewish remnant, who fought on even after the Temple had been destroyed. And a most exciting discovery was the actual Cardo which crossed the ancient city from the present Damascus Gate to a gate in the southern wall, not far from the present Zion Gate. This wide central avenue is lined with columns as depicted in the sixth-century Madeba map.[8] The visitor to Jerusalem can now walk down the restored Cardo and experience the feel of Jerusalem in Roman times.

Overshadowing the explorations in the Jewish Quarter have been those near the Temple Mount. Two items may suffice as examples. For more than a century, tourists and students have been shown the famous Robinson's Arch jutting out from the western wall of the Temple Mount,

7. See p. 52.
8. See p. 43.

south of the Wailing Wall. Professor Edward Robinson claimed that this arch supported a bridge connecting the Temple Mount with the Upper City, which is now the Jewish Quarter. His reasoning was logical and he found support in Josephus' works. But it has now been proven by archeologists digging in the area, that Robinson's Arch supported a stairway from the Temple Mount to the Tyropean Valley below. Another of the exciting discoveries was the broad stairway on the southern side of the Temple Wall, by means of which the pilgrims in ancient times ascended to the Huldah Gate leading to the Temple Mount. The pilgrim psalms that are introduced with the phrase "A song of ascents" probably refer to these ascending steps where these songs of praise were sung by the pilgrims. The content of the psalms fits the situation admirably.

Jerusalem has changed hands many times, but never has a change in Jerusalem's sovereignty brought with it a new birth such as occurred in 1967, when the city was reunited. Sir Ronald Storrs and C.R. Ashbee could not have visualized these activities and these achievements.

No sooner was the city reunited, than a new town planning scheme was initiated. Both the central government and the Jerusalem municipality pursued a program aimed at preserving the precious monuments and developing the united city, plans that have been implemented with vigor and determination.

One of the painful points in dispute that has plagued the Jews for many generations has been the place of worship at the Western or Wailing Wall. The place next to the Wailing Wall was merely a narrow blind alley, eleven feet in width, with a total area of 120 square yards. Only a few dozen people could squeeze into it for worship. Bordering the area was a slum known as Moghrabi. Access to the area of worship was gained through a narrow lane on the north. Chairs, even for the sick and aged, were strictly forbidden. In 1839, during the Egyptian occupation of Jerusalem, the

British Consul informed Ibrahim Pasha, the Egyptian commander in chief of the occupying army, that a British Jew had made a bequest for paving the strip in front of the wall. The consul asked that the Jews be permitted to undertake the work. Ibrahim Pasha was inclined to grant permission. But the strenuous opposition of the Moslems led to a denial, on the grounds that the area adjoins the wall of the Haram al-Sharif as well as the place of the tethering of Buraq. The Jews, he contended, must be warned against raising their voices and other ostentations. They are only allowed their visits as before was his decree.

In May 1918, Chaim Weizmann wrote to Lord Balfour and asked permission to acquire the derelict houses in front of the Western or Wailing Wall. "We are willing," wrote Weizman, "to compensate this community very liberally. We should like to give it a dignified and respectable appearance." The attempt to purchase these hovels came to naught. The Arabs refused to enter into negotiations, the matter was dropped, and the condition of the Wall remained the same. After the riots of 1929, the Jews again proposed the purchase of the hovels and the cleansing of the area so that it be a credit to the holy place. Again the Arabs were violently opposed.

On June 7, 1967 the Old City was captured by the Israeli forces and the hovels in front of the Wall were immediately cleared away. The inhabitants of the slum were relocated in livable residences and reimbursed. The cleared area became a place of worship for thousands of Jews, especially on the Ninth of Av, the anniversary of the fall of Jerusalem to the Babylonians, and again to the Romans. Who gave the order to remove these hovels, no one seems to know. A blight was removed, and in its place, there is an attractive plaza. But the Jerusalem plan for the Western or Wailing Wall area is more ambitious. One of its provisions calls for lowering the street level in front of the Wall to its original base, which will reveal the Wall as it was in the days of King Herod, about twice its present height.

On the hill facing the Western Wall of the Old City, across the Valley of Hinnom, old almshouses were erected through the agency of Moses Montefiore in 1856. They were called Mishkenot Sha'ananim (Dwellings of Tranquility). These dilapidated and decrepit buildings were now restored and a lovely park landscaped around them, with flower beds, paths, and benches tastefully arranged. These houses now serve as Jerusalem's guest houses for artists and for men and women of renown from all over the world. In the years since they were opened in 1973, these buildings have been host to over a thousand foreign writers, artists, musicians, and scholars, who have stayed there and done their creative work "under the shadow" of Jerusalem's old walls. The guests are not obliged to "create" while they are staying at Mishkenot Sha'ananim, but their creative genius is usually inspired by the incomparable view of the Holy City from this hillside.

What would have most delighted the planners of the Mandatory period is the realization of what they had regarded as only a messianic hope—the "green belt" around the Old City. This dream is fast becoming a reality, due in large measure to the energetic and imaginative drive of Jerusalem's long term mayor, Teddy Kollek. The project is now called the Jerusalem National Park. It will be recalled that the plan was originally developed in the days of the Pro-Jerusalem Council. After the Six-Day War, the city planners revived the idea of a green belt around the Old City. Mr. Kollek involved himself intensely in fund-raising efforts and succeeded in raising millions of dollars for this imaginative "green belt." A substantial part of the Jerusalem National Park has already been completed, especially on the western side of the Old City. It includes a vast underground parking lot to make the Old City more accessible to pilgrims and tourists, yet preserve the beauty and serenity of the area surrounding the Walls. Thus the "gory Vale of Hinnom" is now a lovely park which contains a large outdoor amphitheater known as the Sultan's Pool, which hosts international performances for thousands of spectators, and boasts a world class motion picture foundation, comprising two theaters and a film archive, known as the Jerusalem Cinemateque.

One of the most substantial contributions to the Jerusalem National Park has come from a group of fundamentalist Christians in Europe and America known as Beth Shalom. Their large contribution financed the section of the green belt next to the southern wall, between the Zion and the Dung gates. That neglected area is now one of the loveliest sections of the Park and includes an archeological garden. Mr. Kollek's successor has continued to vigorously implement these farsighted policies.

The task of preserving the character of the Old City and, at the same time, developing the modern city is difficult and challenging. While some are vociferous in their outcry against any development that mars in the slightest degree the surrounding landscape, there are others who clamor for the development of the suburbs as a modern metropolis with commerce and industry. The lot of a mayor who is dedicated both to the preservation of the religious, cultural, and historic uniqueness of the Holy City and, at the same time, willing to forge ahead with the expansion of the city's modernization as a living home for hundreds of thousands of inhabitants is not an easy one.

Building on the foundations laid by the British Mandatory government, the municipality, in cooperation with other agencies, including the government of Israel, undertook the program of planning Jerusalem's development. Some of the world's most reputable city planners, architects, archeologists, and scholars were enlisted in the work of planning Jerusalem's future. It is the hope of the municipality that the Holy City will, at one and the same time, preserve and restore the sacred monuments and expand the New City, as a modern metropolis, in harmony with the old.

Jerusalem is a city situated at the crossroads of continents. As such, through the centuries, its streets have resounded with the tread of conquerors. Many are the representatives of mighty empires that have raised their flags over the city, only to depart, never to return as the tides of empire recede. Only the Jews come back, again and again. To them, it is not an outpost of empire. To them, it is their ancestral home, their Sacred City, one and unique. They have come not as empire builders, but in answer to the call of "Mother Zion." Is this the Will of God, or, as the secularists would say, a matter of destiny? Be that as it may, Jerusalem is now a united city, the flourishing capital of the State of Israel. It is enjoying an enlightened and liberal government. Its spiritual and historic monuments are well cared for, and its holy places are protected and accessible. Economic and cultural standards have risen greatly, and the city has experienced an unprecedented growth. What troubles the inhabitants as well as the friends of the Holy City everywhere is the city's uncertain future. There are dark clouds hovering over Jerusalem. Those who love Jerusalem and are concerned for its future are pondering the words of the Hebrew prophet:

O you, the Lord's remembrancers,
Take no rest.
And give no rest to Him,
Until He establish Jerusalem
And make her renowned on earth. (Isa. 62:6–7).

Epilogue

Jerusalem Today and Tomorrow

Sir Ronald Storrs says in his memoirs that "there was not, when I took over, one single private car or telephone in Jerusalem."[1] This was in December 1917. Today, Jerusalem is confronted with massive automobile congestion and possesses a state-of-the-art digitalized telephone system. The city now has over half a million inhabitants and draws, in addition, on a large suburban population as well. This reality reflects the unprecedented growth of the city during the last few decades and the revolutionary changes that have taken place in a very short time. Yet, how little has the Holy City really changed! With all the modernity and the vast expansion, one can still trace the city's ancient history, especially its sacred elements, with great accuracy. The pilgrims can still walk in the footsteps of their prophets and saints as they have for many centuries. Despite mod-

---

1. Ronald Storrs, *Orientations* (London: Nicholson and Watson, 1937), 343.

195

ernity and growth, Jerusalem has not lost its unique charm.

There was a time when the Old City was the whole of Jerusalem. Outside the walls, there were only rocky hills where bands of robbers roamed freely. At night, the gates of Jerusalem were closed till sunrise. Today, a glance at Jerusalem's map reveals a sprawling metropolis outside the city walls. A New City envelops the Old City, so that the Jerusalem of the mid-nineteenth century is now a mere enclave within the greater city that has grown up outside the walls. Yet the Old City, surrounded by its massive walls and towers, is still the core of Jerusalem; its traditional uniqueness is still preserved; and it is still a source of wonder and inspiration for pilgrims and tourists. "Immutability," said Eliot Warburton in the mid-nineteenth century, "is the most striking characteristic of the East; from the ancient strife of Cain and Abel to the present struggle between the Crescent and the Cross, the people remain in their habits of thought and action less changed than the countries they inhabit."[2] These words were uttered before Jerusalem was catapulted into modernity. Yet one can still repeat these words with a large measure of relevancy. Within the rapid changes of the recent decades, there is still a measure of immutability, especially in regard to the city's sancta. To be sure, there have been changes even in the Old City. But never have the sancta themselves been marred by modern development and growth. Thus the offensive smells that used to characterize the Old City bazaars and alleys are gone. The open sewers have been replaced by a modern sewage system. The Jewish Quarter, which was the most derelict of the Old City slums, has been tastefully and attractively restored and the stinking Moghrabi slum next

---

2. Eliot Warburton, *The Crescent and the Cross* (London: H. Colburn, 1845), Vol. 1, p. v.

to the Western or Wailing Wall has been replaced by a large plaza where masses of Jews gather for prayer and festive celebrations. Yet the Old City has retained its aura of sanctity, the shrines have remained inviolate, and they continue to inspire reverence and piety.

Many nineteenth century writers on the theme of Jerusalem bewail the new neighborhoods that have grown up outside the city walls. They often tell how deeply moved were the pilgrims by the sight of the city rising up in the midst of total desolation and emptiness. The pilgrims would suddenly behold, from the distance, the grey walls, battlements, and towers of the Holy City issuing out of the bare and rocky hills of Judea. This first sight of Jerusalem was indeed a soul-stirring and unforgettable experience. It awakened holy sentiments even in the hearts of hardened skeptics. But one can find comfort in the thought that modernity has spoiled only the first view of the Holy City; and that, from a distance. The fact is that the Old City, with its massive walls and towers, now stunningly illuminated by night, has been preserved, and the New City contains many new cultural and spiritual assets that more than compensate for the thrilling first glimpse of Jerusalem's ramparts, which still rise up before the visitor as he approaches the "green belt" surrounding them. Jerusalem has ceased to be a museum of shrines and holy places. It is now a living city which lovingly preserves and cares for the shrines, monuments, and holy places which are sacred to its own inhabitants and to millions throughout the world.

Jerusalem has changed in many ways, but its unique charm has not diminished. A romantic tourist once complained that the New City is too modern. Teddy Kollek, then Jerusalem's mayor, is reported to have responded: "You ride to your office in a Buick, but you expect me to ride to my office on a donkey!" Development and change are inherent in the process of life. Jerusalem is a living city; it has grown and expanded; but its growth has been carefully watched and lovingly guided so that its sanctity and its charm have not been marred by the insensitivity of builders and the vulgarity of developers. Greed has not been allowed to determine the nature of Jerusalem's growth. This sacred task has been entrusted to a planning commission that is in touch with some of the world's outstanding city planners. Jerusalem's development seems to be in good hands, and it will probably continue to be guided with responsibility and discriminating taste.

Politically, too, Jerusalem has changed beyond recognition. In 1877, when George Adam Smith published his classic work on *Jerusalem*, the city was still . . .

> . . . a small provincial town in the hinterland of a derelict Turkish empire—the "Sick Man of Europe"—riddled with corruption and inefficiency, overburdened by an enormous external debt to which its income had been mortgaged, and tottering under a regime of indecision that stultified any attempt at reform and regeneration.

Now as the twentieth century draws to a close, Jerusalem is:

> . . . [the] capital of a small but dynamic independent republic, a modern metropolis pulsing with economic and cultural vigor, and looking forward to still greater achievements.[3]

Needless to say, Israel progressed from autocracy to democracy, from Eastern deviousness and restriction to Western freedom and rule of law. The glowing words above were written in 1972. Today, the external situation has changed radically, and Jerusalem's political future is not as secure and its fortunes are again a matter of concern.

---

3. Samuel Yeiven, "Prolegomenon" in *Jerusalem* by George Adam Smith (Hoboken, NJ: KTAV Publishing House, 1972), XXXVI.

Reasons for Hope and for Concern

On the Day of Atonement of 1973 (October 6), when everything was calm and peaceful, and most of Jerusalem's Jewish inhabitants were in the synagogue at prayer, the shattering call was heard for all men of military age to leave for the battlefield. The Egyptians and Syrians had launched an unprovoked war. In the first three days, while Israel was mobilizing its forces, the Arabs managed to make substantial advances. The Egyptians crossed the Suez Canal; the Syrians penetrated deep into the Golan Heights. These initial victories were of short duration. The Israeli army crossed the Suez Canal and encircled the Egyptian army. The Syrians were not only pushed out of the Golan Heights, but the Israeli army penetrated deep into Syrian territory. As in previous occasions, the United States and the Soviet Union intervened and saved the Syrians and Egyptians from a humiliating defeat. Later, Israel was forced to withdraw to its prewar positions.

This war, like the Six-Day War before it, had been made possible, if not actually instigated, by the Soviet Union. It was Russia who had provided the political backing to Israel's enemies, as well as the mountains of arms that had enabled Egypt and Syria to launch their attack. The Soviet Union, in supporting the Arabs, had engineered for itself a no-lose situation: if the Arabs won, Russia would get the credit; if the Arabs lost, they would need even more resupply and support. Win or lose, with each war the Arab states would become ever more dependent on their patron, and the Soviet Union would become ever more entrenched in the Middle East.

General Anwar al-Sadat, Nasser's successor as President of Egypt, realized this only too well. Determined to end a dependence upon the USSR that amounted to vassaldom, he set escape from the embrace of Russia as his overriding goal. In July 1972, shortly before he launched his assault on Israel, he expelled Soviet advisors from Egypt, thus giving himself a free hand. In March 1976, he unilaterally abrogated the Egyptian-Soviet Treaty of Friendship and Cooperation. In the summer of 1977, he stopped shipping cotton to Russia and, at the end of that September, he stopped repayment on the four-billion dollar debt owed to the USSR for two decades of military supplies. Sadat had succeeded in escaping the clutches of the Russian bear. Indeed, this break with the Soviet Union and subsequent reorientation of Egypt to the West was, in the long term, probably Sadat's most monumental and lasting accomplishment for the Egyptian people.

One can then imagine his shock and chagrin upon reading the Soviet-American Declaration of October 1, 1977, announcing their agreement to reconvene the Geneva Conference under joint American and Soviet chairmanship, with the clear intention of imposing a comprehensive superpower settlement on the Middle East. This would bring the Russians back under circumstances that would make it well nigh impossible for Egypt ever again to free itself. At all costs, the reconvened Geneva Conference had to be sidetracked.

For Sadat, ever the audacious gambler, this meant dramatically seizing the initiative from out of the hands of the superpowers. He would go to Jerusalem and personally break the deadlock between Israel and Egypt!

On November 9, 1977, Sadat announced to his Parliament that he was ready "to go to the ends of the earth. Israel will be astonished when it hears me saying now, before you, that I am ready to go to their own house, to the Knesset itself, to talk to them." Israel was astounded. Since 1948, Israel had been insisting on direct, face to face, negotiations with the Arabs. The Arabs had always refused, for this would imply recognition of Israel. Thus, Sadat's offer was revolutionary—if he meant it. Two days later, on

November 11, the Prime Minister of Israel, Menahem Begin, in an unprecedented speech addressed directly to the Egyptian people, accepted the challenge:

> Citizens of Egypt! . . . you are neighbors and always will be . . . Let us say to each other, and let this be the silent vow between our two nations: no more wars, no more threats. . . . It will be a pleasure to welcome and receive your President with the traditional hospitality you and we have inherited from our common father Abraham.[4]

That same evening Begin announced to Egypt and the world: "In the name of the government of Israel, I officially invite the President of Egypt to come to Jerusalem. *Ahalan wa Sahalan,*" he concluded in Arabic: Welcome.[5]

> *Hu higiah.* With the Hebrew words for "He's arrived," commentator Yaakov Ahimeir told three million Israelis that it was not a dream . . . At 7.59 P.M. on the evening of November 19, after a brief flight from Abu Sweir airbase, the Boeing 707, code-signed Egypt 01, touched down at Ben-Gurion Airport, not far from Tel Aviv. . . . The motorcade, lights blazing, sirens howling, swept up the broad, steep highway to Jerusalem. As it wound through the streets of the city, thousands lined the pavements to cheer it on its way; mothers held their infants aloft to catch a glimpse of the visitor. . . . At the King David Hotel the manager welcomed President Sadat with certificates testifying that 180 trees had been planted in his name in the Jerusalem Peace Forest.[6]

The following day, November 20, 1977, after worshipping in the Al-Aqsa Mosque on the Temple Mount, and

---

4. As quoted in David Hirst and Irene Beeson, *Sadat* (London: Faber and Faber Ltd., 1981), pp. 258–259.
5. *Ibid.*, p. 260.
6. *Ibid.*, pp. 264–266.

paying pro forma visits to the Church of the Holy Sepulchre and the Yad Vashem Holocaust Memorial, Sadat
addressed a special session of Israel's parliament, the
Knesset. Here he laid down, as a condition of peace, the
redivision of Jerusalem:

> "There are facts that should be faced with all courage and
> clarity. There are Arab territories which Israel has occupied
> and still occupies by armed force. We insist upon complete
> withdrawal from these territories, including Arab Jeru-
> salem. . . . Let me tell you without the slightest hesitation,
> that I have not come to you under this roof to request that
> your troops evacuate the occupied territories. Complete
> withdrawal from the Arab territories occupied in 1967 is a
> logical and undisputed fact. . . . this is a foregone conclu-
> sion, which is not open to discussion or debate. I have come
> to Jerusalem, the City of Peace, which will always remain as
> a living embodiment of coexistence among believers of the
> three religions. It is inadmissable that anyone should
> conceive the special status of the City of Jerusalem within
> the framework of annexation or expansionism. It should be
> a free and open city for all believers. . . ."[7]

Begin, in his reply, reminded Sadat and the Arab world
that the Land of Israel and the Old City of Jerusalem is the
homeland of the Jewish people: Here ". . . we created our
civilization, and our Prophets had their visions, and their
sanctified words stand until this day. Here the Kings of
Israel and Judah worshipped. Here we became a people."
Then, addressing the concerns Sadat had raised in his
speech, Begin continued:

> "Mr. President, allow me to say a word about Jerusalem.
> You prayed today at a place of worship sanctified to Islam.

---

7. As quoted in *Sadat in Jerusalem, November 19–21, 1977, Souve-
nir Album* (Jerusalem: The Jerusalem Post, 1979), 38.

And from there we went to the Church of the Holy Sepulchre. You have seen, as all the world knows, that ever since
this has become a city joined together there is absolutely
free access, without hindrance, for members of every faith
to their Holy Sites. This was not the case during nineteen
years (of Arab occupation). It has existed for some eleven
years (since 1967), and we can assure the world of Islam
and the Christian world, we can assure all the nations that
there will always be free access to the holy places of every
faith. We shall defend this right of free access because we
believe in the equality of the rights of man and respect for
every faith."[8]

Thus, in the midst of, and despite the euphoria of the
moment, both sides staked out their positions with regard
to Jerusalem.

Just forty-four hours after he had touched down at
Ben-Gurion Airport, Sadat took off for Egypt. He had
succeeded in breaking the deadlock, and in torpedoing the
Geneva Conference. Israel and Egypt would negotiate
directly. After a year and a half, they would arrive at a
peace treaty. But this treaty would require Sadat to back
down from his demands for Jerusalem. Sadat put the
interests of Egypt first: full diplomatic relations in return
for all of the Sinai peninsula. The issue of Jerusalem had
been raised. It had not been settled, only deferred. In the
meantime, the now uneasy status quo continued.

Anwar al-Sadat was a brave and a bold man. He led
Egypt on a new path to the West and opened the possibility
for an era of peace in the Middle East. But there was a
price to pay. By traveling to Jerusalem to make a separate
peace with Israel, by putting Egypt's parochial interests
first, abandoning the Arab world and, in effect, concurring
in Jerusalem's unified status under Israeli rule, Sadat

---

8. *Ibid.*, p. 40.

earned the designation of traitor in the eyes of many devout Moslems and Pan-Arab nationalists. On October 6, 1981, the bill was presented.

On that day, the anniversary, according to the Gregorian Calendar, of Sadat's launching of the Egyptian army across the Suez Canal eight years before, a great parade was held in Cairo to commemorate the beginning of the war. But to Lt. Khalid Hassan Shafiq Islambouli, a calendar promulgated by a Pope and used by the secular world was irrelevant. To Shafiq and his band of fanatic Moslems, this day, according to the *Islamic Calendar*, was *Id al-Adha*, the anniversary of Sadat's dramatic trip to Jerusalem four years before. On this anniversary, Islamic justice would be executed upon the traitor. In a hail of bullets, Sadat, in his resplendent uniform of blue and gold with a sash of sacred green, was cut down on the reviewing stand. The bold visionary was no more.

His successor, General Hosni Mubarak, was not Sadat. He had been among the leaders within the Egyptian establishment opposing Sadat's peace treaty with Israel. Now, having inherited a fait accompli, he whittled the peace down to its barest minimum: formal diplomatic relations but the absolute minimum of cultural, economic, or personal contacts. Egypt now, once again, became the chief spokesman of Sadat's original position, that Jerusalem's return to pre-1967 status was the key to any Arab–Israeli peace. Once again confrontation became the order of the day, and in the confrontation between the Arabs and the Jews, Jerusalem was the major prize. Not only is the city both the holiest city in Judaism and the third holiest city in Islam, but the capital of Jewish Israel is seen by Arabs as the potential capital of an Arab Palestinian State. The future of Jerusalem was right back on the table.

A deep pessimism has gripped the hearts of many observers. Would Jerusalem the Holy once again become a pawn in the game of political expediency, to be traded in obedience to the dictates of one powerful interest or another? They ask, in the words of the prophet: "Watchman, what of the night? Watchman, what of the night?" Most of the Jews who dwell in the Holy City are not as frightened as those who see the problem from afar. Some rest their confidence on faith. They see political pressures as transient trends, and respond to the prophetic question in the words of the same prophet:

> Hatch a plot—it shall be foiled;
> Agree on action—it shall not succeed,
> For God is with us. (Isa. 8:10).

Rather than focus on the immediate and political, they focus on what makes Jerusalem unique among all the cities of the earth. This significance, they feel, will ultimately overide all political pressures. And so they take comfort in the words of the Prophet:

> Be glad and rejoice forever in that which I create;
> For behold, I create Jerusalem a rejoicing,
> And her people a joy. . . .
> They shall not build and another inhabit,
> They shall not plant and another eat . . .
> They shall not labor in vain . . . (Isa. 65:18,22–23).

The Futility of Plans to Internationalize or Partition the City

The realists in Jerusalem analyze the alternative prospects, and are equally confident of Jerusalem's future. They start with Jerusalem's uniqueness, which has created for it unique and painful problems. Jerusalem is unique not only because of its long and dramatic history, but mainly because its history has had a powerful impact on the life of so many nations both near and far. The city's destiny has become a pivot of international concern and involvement. Jerusalem has become, for many, a city apart from the land and the people, and it is treated as a special "problem." While the land can be governed by the people who live in it, Jerusalem, they say, should be an international enclave governed by an international agency. This, indeed, has been the position of the United States State Department since 1947. Unfortunately, they gloss over the historic fact that such an agency had already governed Jerusalem and the whole of Palestine for three decades. The British Mandatory Government was an international agency which governed by virtue of the Mandate that it received from the League of Nations. That international agency proved a failure because the inhabitants, both Arabs and Jews, rejected foreign agencies as their rulers. If the internationalized Jerusalem were to be entrusted to a commission, Jerusalem would surely become the breeding ground for political intrigue, which would rob the city of any chance of peace and harmony among the religious communities.

People who propose that Jerusalem should be internationalized do not take into account the living reality, that the people who dwell in Jerusalem regard their city as a place of habitation as well as a city of shrines and holy places. Some romantic visitors have looked upon the introduction by the Israeli government of electricity, running water, street lighting, and sewers in the Old City as rank desecration and defilement of the Holy City. And profanity of profanities—modern transportation—absolutely scandalous. Walking in the dark alleys with a lantern is, to some people, a sacred ritual, and smelling the stench of the open sewers is no less than sweet-smelling incense. And the patient little donkeys as the city's public conveyances are so quaint and romantic! Weren't they used by the apostles? And, by contrast, what can be more satanic than a convenient bus? Norman Macleod in his excellent book, *Eastward*, related a nineteenth century incident that is still typical of many a romantic visitor in Jerusalem.

> I remember a lady, whose mind was engrossed with the question of the return of the Jews to Palestine, being dreadfully shocked by a religious and highly respectable man, who presumed to express the opinion in her hearing, that the time was not far distant when there might be a railway from Jaffa to Jerusalem, and the cry be heard from an English voice of, "Bethlehem Station!" The fair friend of Israel thereupon drew herself up indignantly and exclaimed, "Pray, sir, don't be profane!" The unfortunate friend of progress went home that night under the impression that, unknown to himself, he had hitherto been an infidel.[9]

Will Jerusalem be internationalized? Judging by the present situation, one can say that this is a very doubtful prospect. Jerusalem is the de facto capital of the State of Israel. As of now, the internationalization plan has been filed away, and has been but sparingly mentioned by the Powers these many years. The Vatican, too, has become less insistent on this plan than it once was.

The realists have also pondered the plan calling for a return to the pre-Six-Day War situation when the city was divided into two sectors, one Arab and one Jewish. This proposal assumes that one can turn back the clock of history. Historians can inform these dreamers that just as the same water never flows twice under a bridge, so does the stream of history not repeat its course. Conditions change and, in Jerusalem, they have changed immensely. During the past decades, the city has expanded in all directions and no longer consists of two distinct sectors, an

---

9. Norman Macleod, *Eastward* (London: A. Strahan, 1866), 117–119.

Arab sector to the east and a Jewish sector to the west. Today, there are as many Jews living in the eastern part of Jerusalem as Arabs. The city has become an integrated and indivisible metropolis. Economically, too, it is hard to visualize either Arabs or Jews agreeing to the construction of a wall to divide the city. Few indeed are those who subscribe to such a Solomonic judgment for Jerusalem. The proposal is more than a quarter of a century out of date.

The Human Aspect of the City's Future

Israel's view in regard to the above proposals was clearly expressed on July 30, 1980. On that day, after extensive debate, the Knesset voted overwhelmingly to declare United Jerusalem, including the Old City, the "Eternal Capital of Israel." This statement reaffirmed Israel's stand that there will be no compromise on united Jerusalem as Israel's capital.

Israel is prepared to negotiate the status of the religious communities and their holy places in Jerusalem. The negotiations, however, must begin with a clear realization that the holy places in Jerusalem and the city of Jerusalem are two separate and distinct issues. Unless these issues are disentangled, confusion, discord, and dissension will continue to plague all negotiations. The confusion of the issues is a carry-over from the Middle Ages when the Crusaders came from afar to do battle with the infidels for the possession of the Holy Sepulchre. This ended with a Christian Kingdom of Jerusalem. But the mentality of modern man is quite different from that of the Middle Ages. Today people approach political problems from the human aspect, and the city of Jerusalem is a metropolis in which more than half a million people live. To be sure, the government of Jerusalem must provide for the city's sancta;

more so than in any other city of the world. However, the sancta are only one aspect, a very important one indeed, but only one of the responsibilities of the government.

The holy places in Jerusalem need a city administration that can be trusted to govern *with due reverence* for the shrines, sacred sites, and traditions of all the religious communities. The city administration must be such that will fully guarantee freedom of access to the holy places and freedom of worship for all the sects, large and small. The religious communities must be granted the right of self-government in all matters pertaining to their churches, mosques, or synagogues, and to the performance of their rituals in accordance with their traditions. In sum, the city of Jerusalem needs an effective administration which can govern with equity, maintain peace, ensure the safety of person and property, and safeguard the rights of the residents, both as individuals and as communities. The Turkish administration during the four centuries of its rule in Jerusalem was unsatisfactory because of the corruption of its city officials. In theory, however, the administrative approach of the central government was, in the main, sound, for it conceived the residents of the Holy City as consisting of a number of coexisting religious communities who governed themselves in accordance with their own religious law. Topping these semi-autonomous communities was a central government that guaranteed these communities their rights and safety. Regretfully, ineptitude and corruption violated these basic tenets of government. The British followed the same principles, with the difference that the administration was not afflicted by corruption and venality. That this governmental approach is sound has been established by historic experience. The city flourished when it was governed as a place of human habitation, and it declined whenever it was administered as a sacred museum, waiting for pilgrims.

Which Governmental Agency Should Administer Jerusalem?

Those who are concerned for Jerusalem's future should ask themselves which agency can be trusted with an equitable administration of Jerusalem. After the British left, the Jordanians took over the government of the Old City. While they provided free access to the Christian holy places, they destroyed nearly all the Jewish religious, philanthropic, and cultural monuments and institutions, and denied the Jews access to their holy places. This departure from the centuries-old tradition in the city was also a clear breach of the pledges in the Armistice Agreement, in which Jordan undertook to give the Jews "free access to the holy places and cultural institutions and the use of the Cemetery on the Mount of Olives." Obviously Jordan, and for that matter any Arab government, cannot be trusted with the administration of Jerusalem. Israel understandably refuses to rely on the pledged word of the Arabs in regard to the control of the Old City.

Equally unreliable is the United Nations as an administrator of the Holy City. The main reason is that the United Nations never saw fit to take note of the Jordanian discrimination against the Jews or of the Jordanian breach of the provisions of the Armistice Agreement.

In contrast, when the Old City came under Israeli control in 1967, an enlightened and liberal administration was immediately established. The city has flourished in every area of human interest. The holy places have been protected, and the faithful of all religious communities have had free access to their shrines, Moslem no less than Christian or Jewish. The Israeli government can therefore point proudly to its record as custodian of the Holy City as proof of its ability to protect the holy places and to its credibility as guarantor of unrestricted freedom of worship for all religions. When former Prime Minister Golda Meir was granted an audience with Pope Paul VI, the pontiff thanked her for the way in which Israel had safeguarded the holy places of Christianity. And the Moslems residing in Jerusalem have not only had full control over the Temple Mount, but they have been free to make pilgrimages to Mecca and Medina, despite the state of war that still formally exists between Israel and Saudi Arabia. Similarly, Christians residing in Moslem countries were granted entry to Israel in order to worship at their holy places.

The Moslem–Jewish controversy over the holy places derives from the fact that both Jews and Moslems have earnest historic claims to Mount Moriah. The Jews call it the Temple Mount, that is, the Mount on which the Holy Temple was erected by King Solomon. The Moslems call it Haram al-Sharif, the Noble Sanctuary. These clashing claims led to riots and bloodshed during the British administration. But since the Jewish capture of the Old City, the situation has been much calmer. A relatively peaceful modus vivendi has replaced the turmoil that existed under the British and the discrimination that prevailed under the Jordanians. Most Jews have limited their claim to the area outside the Temple compound, in front of the Western (Wailing) wall. The Temple Mount itself, they have left for the Messianic era, which does not seem to be at hand. They want to assemble unmolested in front of the Wall for worship and other relevant celebrations. The Arabs do not worship in front of the Wall. They assign sanctity to the other side of the Wall where Muhammad's miraculous steed was tethered. All this lends itself to a simple Solomonic judgment. The Jews will have their side of the Wall and the Moslems the other side. When the Messianic era comes, the whole issue will be reconsidered.

Jews and Arabs should be encouraged to enhance and beautify their respective sides of the Wall without encroaching on each other's sacred sites. Were the issue

purely religious, the above solution might work, as it has
already worked during the past decades. Unfortunately,
political considerations have complicated the problem. No
one can, therefore, predict the future. One can only "pray
for the peace of Jerusalem" (Ps. 122:6).

Israel's liberal policy has been based partly on enlightened self-interest, but more so on the Jewish cultural
tradition. Dr. Saul Colbi, in his *Christianity in the Holy
Land, Past and Present*, emphasizes this aspect of Israel's
credibility with clarity and discernment. He writes:

> In Israel, at all events, there are indestructible factors that
> safeguard Christian interests. Though geographically in
> Asia, Israel is firmly linked with the civilization of the West.
> Willingly, and from a deep sense of cultural and conceptual
> affinity, it finds itself drawn naturally into friendships and
> exchanges with the West. But the continuity of the Chris-
> tians of Israel as an inviolable and self-determining group,
> ethnic and religious, depends in largest part upon Juda-
> ism's immemorial hospitality and kindness towards the
> stranger (as the Bible teaches it), on Israel's fundamental
> democracy, on the Jewish aversion to win proselytes.[10]

In the clash of conflicting nationalisms, religious and
historical arguments are often utilized in support of the
respective political goals. In regard to Jerusalem, however,
the most relevant factors are the emotional attachments of
the disputing parties to the city. The historic and religious
experiences of the past are important only to the extent of
their impact on the consciousness of the present generation. Symbolic articulations based on national memories,
however sacred these rituals may be, can determine political decisions only to the extent that they affect the emo-

---

10. Saul Colbi, *Christianity in the Holy Land, Past and Present* (Tel
Aviv: Am Hasefer Publishing House, 1969), 201.

tional attachments of the people to the objects of those symbolic rituals.

The depth of the emotional attachment of the Jewish people to Jerusalem is almost unfathomable! The plaintive oath of the ancient Jews who were led into captivity more than 2,500 years ago has continued to echo in the hearts of Jews of every generation:

If I forget thee, O Jerusalem,
Let my right hand forget its cunning,
Let my tongue cleave to the roof of my mouth,
If I remember thee not;
If I set not Jerusalem
Above my chiefest joy. (Ps. 137:5–6).

The intent of this national oath has been reiterated at every Jewish birth, marriage, and burial service. However, as stated above, it is not the ritual that establishes Israel's claim to the Holy City. It is the vow of modern Israel to shed its blood rather than abandon Jerusalem that carries the weight of conviction. One can conclude with a fair degree of certainty that Israel will negotiate on the holy places, but not on Jerusalem.

Jerusalem's Promising Future Under Israel's Administration

Despite these forceful considerations, one cannot predict with any certainty the future of Jerusalem, a city that is holy to many peoples and is a precious prize for contending, empire-building nations. However, one can predict a bright future for the Holy City if it is allowed to continue to be administered by the enlightened policies that have characterized the Israeli administration during the recent past. Given peace with the neighboring Arab states, and the current enlightened administration of Israel, Jerusa-

lem and its religious communities can anticipate a state of
harmonious, peaceful, and cooperative coexistence, with
each community serving God according to its own theology and tradition.

Since the reunification of the city, the Israeli government
and the municipality of Jerusalem have focused their
attention on a practical course of action. A town planning
team was set up to develop a comprehensive scheme in
accordance with which the city is to be rebuilt from its
ruins, restored to its authentic self, and beautified so that
it will no longer be known as "that melancholy city."[11] In
1973, the city planning team published its plan. In a
moving Foreword to the volume, the author, Arieh Sharon,
describes the reverent approach of the planning team to its
challenging task. A couple of paragraphs from the Foreword will give the reader a glimpse at the grand scale and
the detailed work that have gone into the Jerusalem Plan.
The author writes:

> There is also a special beauty about the Old City of
> Jerusalem, the wondrous beauty of a city set amidst the
> timeless terraces and hills of Judea, perched on hillocks,
> surrounded by magnificent stone ramparts, skirted by
> ravines and faced by the gentle slopes of the Mount of
> Olives and Mount Scopus with their commanding view of
> the plain of Jericho, the Jordan River and the Dead Sea.
> How does one preserve this beauty, yet provide modern
> amenities for a growing population and for the hundreds of
> thousands of annual visitors who are drawn to this centre
> of pilgrimage in increasing numbers?

> To conserve the old and bring forth the full measure of its
> magnificence; to conceive the new with a sense of history so

---

11. W. H. Bartlett, when leaving Jerusalem at the end of his first
pilgrimage, referred to the city as "the melancholy city," and melancholy it was indeed in the year 1842.

that it blends with its ancient surroundings; and to enhance
and add a dimension to the special character of this city of
antiquity and scenic beauty—these were the challenges
presented to the Jerusalem town planners. . . .[12]

With this quotation from the Foreword to the Jerusalem
City Plan, it is hoped that those who are concerned for
Jerusalem will make an effort to learn about the imaginative concepts concerning Jerusalem's future that Israel
means to turn into reality. Israel means to develop Jerusalem in accordance with a broad planning concept involving the city's walls and gates, holy places and shrines, and
the living quarters and institutions within the Old City and
the surrounding areas. "Jerusalem," said Rabbi Yohanan, a
Talmudic sage, "will one day become the metropolis of the
whole earth" (Ex. R. 23:10). Obviously, Jerusalem is not
destined to become the biggest city in the world, but it may
be destined to become the greatest city. A city's greatness is
measured not in square miles, but by its exemplary institutions, its priceless monuments, and the nobility of its
aspirations. Jerusalem, it is hoped, will, one day, really
become the spiritual metropolis of the world: "For out of
Zion will go forth Torah, and the word of the Lord from
Jerusalem" (Isa. 2:3).

---

12. Arieh Sharon, *Planning Jerusalem: The Old City and Its Environs*
(London: Weidenfeld and Nicolson, 1973), iii.

Glossary

Aelia Capitolina: The name of Jerusalem when the Romans rebuilt it as a pagan city.

Al-Aqsa Mosque: The mosque in the southern section of the Temple Mount.

Anastasia: The section of the Church of the Holy Sepulchre where Jesus' tomb is located.

Ashkenazi: A Jew whose origin is traced to West, Central, or Eastern Europe.

Bakshish: A gift of money or graft.

Balfour Declaration: The statement of policy issued by Lord Arthur James Balfour on behalf of the British government on November 2, 1917, pledging British support for the establishment of a national home for the Jewish people in Palestine.

B.C.E.: Before the Common Era.

C.E.: The Common Era.

Coenaculum: The room on Mount Zion where the traditional Last Supper took place.

Dar al-Islam: The "realm of the faithful," territory brought under the political control of Islam during one of its periodic waves of conquest. It is a Moslem principle that a territory once under Islamic political control must remain so forever. It may not revert to non-Moslem control, and should it do so, it must be reclaimed, by force if needs be. See *Jihad*.

Diaspora: The lands of the "dispersion" of the Jews.

Dragoman: An interpreter or guide employed by tourists in the Near East.

Drang nach Osten: "Drive to the East"; the name of the German Medieval policy of expansionism, largely spearheaded by the Knights of the Teutonic Order, later applied to the expansionist Eastern policy of Wilhelmian and later Nazi Germany.

Ecce Homo Arch: The arch in the Via Dolorosa, from which Pilate reputedly said to the crowd below: "Ecce homo" (Behold the man), and thus handed over Jesus to be crucified.

El Kuds: "The Holy" City; the Arabic name for Jerusalem.

Hallel: Psalms 113–118 recited by Jews during certain festivals.

Halutz: A Jewish pioneer, especially a member of a kibbutz.

Hanukkah: The eight day Jewish festival commemorating the victory of the Maccabees over Antiochus Epiphanes and the rededication of the Temple in 165 B.C.E.

Haram al-Sharif: "The Noble Sanctuary"; the Arab name for the Temple Mount where once stood the Temple of Solomon. It now harbors the Dome of the Rock and the Al-Aqsa Mosque.

Hassidim: Ultra-Orthodox Jews who stress sentiment and emotion in worship and are dedicated to certain holy men as their religious leaders.

Holocaust: The systematic and methodical destruction of the European Jewish community by the Nazis during the Second World War.

Hospitallers: A religious military order established in the Crusader Kingdom of Jerusalem in the twelfth century.

Imam: A prayer leader in a mosque.

Janissaries: A former elite corps of Ottoman troops drawn mainly from young Christian boys seized or purchased, converted, and trained as professional Turkish soldiers.

Jihad: Moslem holy war against the infidels. The conquest of infidel territory converts it into part of the *Dar al-Islam*.

Judenrein: The Nazi term for an area from which all Jews had been eliminated.

Kaffiyeh: An Arab headdress, consisting of a square cloth held on the head by a black band.

Karaites: A Jewish sect that accepts only biblical legislation.

Kibbutz: A commune in Israel whose economy was originally based on agriculture, but lately also on industry.

Knesset: Parliament of the State of Israel.

Kohanim: Hebrew word for priests.

Madeba Map: A sixth century mosaic map of Jerusalem and its environs when the city still retained the characteristics of the Roman city of Aelia Capitolina.

Madrassah: A Moslem college of religious studies.

Mameluke: A member of a former elite Egyptian military class drawn mainly from young Christian boys who were purchased as slaves, converted to Islam, and trained as professional soldiers. Eventually, they seized the throne and ruled Egypt from 1250 to 1517.

Mandate, Palestine: The responsibility that the League of Nations conferred on Great Britain in 1922 to administer Palestine in accordance with the aims of the *Balfour Declaration*.

Millet: A community in the Ottoman empire made up of members of a given religious faith, organized under a religious head of its own who also exercised some civil functions.

Muezzin: A Moslem crier who calls the faithful to prayer from the mosque's minaret.

Noble Sanctuary: The enclosure on Mount Moriah, constructed by Herod, where the Dome of the Rock and the Al-Aqsa Mosque are located. See *Haram al-Sharif*.

Orthodox Jews: Jews who strictly observe the laws and traditions of rabbinic Judaism.

Pasha: Turkish title of honor, usually referring to the governor of a city or province.

Sakhra: The Holy Rock within the Dome of the Rock.

Sanhedrin: A body of Jewish scholars who constituted the supreme legislative and judicial body of the Jewish people before the fall of the state in 70 c.e.

Saracens: Nomadic people from the desert between Syria and Arabia; often used as a synonym for Arabs.

Sephardi: A Jew whose origin is traced to Spain or Portugal; also an Oriental Jew.

Six-Day War: The Arab-Israel war of 1967 in which Israel defeated the Egyptian, Syrian, and Jordanian armies in only six days.

Key Dates in Jerusalem's History

B.C.E.

1050	David establishes his kingdom in Jerusalem
1007	Solomon's Temple is dedicated
977	The northern tribes of Israel secede
721	Northern kingdom is destroyed by the Assyrians
586	Babylonians destroy Jerusalem and burn the Temple
536	Cyrus, King of Persia, permits the Jews to return to Jerusalem and rebuild the Temple
516	Second Temple is consecrated
444	Nehemiah rebuilds the walls of Jerusalem
331	Jerusalem surrenders to Alexander the Great
167	Antiochus IV desecrates the Temple
164	The Maccabees rededicate the Temple
63	Pompey captures Jerusalem
37	Herod the Great becomes king

C.E.

41	Herod Agrippa starts the construction of the Third Wall
66	Jewish revolt against Rome begins
70	Romans capture Jerusalem and destroy the Temple
135	Hadrian crushes the Bar Kokhba revolt, destroys Jerusalem, and then rebuilds it as a pagan city

223

324	Constantine becomes master of the Holy Land
325	Jerusalem, now a Christian city, is visited by St. Helena
363	Emperor Julian (the Apostate) initiates the rebuilding of the Temple
614	Chosroes II, king of Persia, sacks and pillages Jerusalem
638	Jerusalem is captured by the Caliph Omar
691	Abd-al-Malik erects the Dome of the Rock
969	Jerusalem comes under the Fatimids of Egypt
1010	The Caliph Hakim destroys the Church of the Holy Sepulchre
1071	The Seljuk Turks conquer Jerusalem
1099	The Crusaders capture Jerusalem
1187	Jerusalem is recaptured by the Moslems under Saladin
1244	The Khorasmian Turks sack Jerusalem and destroy the Church of the Holy Sepulchre
1250	Jerusalem comes under Mameluke rule
1260	The Mongol hordes are driven out and the Mamelukes annex Jerusalem
1267	Rabbi Moses ben Nahman (RaMBaN) settles in Jerusalem
1291	The last of the Latin Kingdoms in the Holy Land falls to the Mamelukes
1517	Jerusalem is captured by the Ottoman Turks
1541	Sultan Suleiman the Magnificent restores the walls of Jerusalem
1700	Judah he-Hasid and his follows arrive in Jerusalem
1799	Napoleon Bonaparte invades the Holy Land
1808	Fire consumes the Church of the Holy Sepulchre
1810	New structure of the Church of the Holy Sepulchre is consecrated

1831	Ibrahim Pasha of Egypt conquers the Holy Land
1838	British consulate is opened in Jerusalem
1840	The Turks are restored to possession of the Holy Land
1843	French and Prussian consulates are opened in Jerusalem
1845	The Greek Orthodox Patriarch of Jerusalem moves from Constantinople to Jerusalem
1847	The Latin Patriarchate is restored in Jerusalem
1853	The Crimean War begins
1856	The first Jewish suburb (Mishkenot Sha'ananim) is built outside the city walls
1862	The United States opens a consulate in Jerusalem
1869	The first road between Jerusalem and Jaffa is contructed
1874	The Me'ah She'arim quarter is established
1881	The American Colony is founded in Jerusalem
1897	The First Zionist Congress is held in Basle, Switzerland
1898	The railway between Jerusalem and Jaffa is built
1917	(November 2) The Balfour Declaration is issued
1917	(December 11) Jerusalem surrenders to the British
1920	The first Arab anti-Jewish outbreak in Jerusalem
1925	(April 1) The Hebrew University on Mount Scopus is dedicated
1936	Arab anti-British and anti-Jewish outbreaks are launched
1939	Second World War begins

1947	United Nations resolves to partition Palestine into Jewish and Arab states
1948	(May 14) The British Mandate is ended
1948	(May 14) Israel's Independence is proclaimed
1948–1949	Israel War of Independence
1948–1967	Jerusalem is a divided city
1949	(December 26) Jerusalem is proclaimed the capital of Israel
1964	Pope Paul VI visits Jerusalem as a pilgrim
1967	(June 5) The Six-Day War begins
1967	(June 7) The Old City is captured by Israeli forces
1967	(June 19) Jerusalem is officially reunited
1973	(October 6) The Yom Kippur War breaks out
1977	(November 20) President Anwar al-Sadat visits Jerusalem
1979	(March 26) Israel–Egypt peace treaty signed
1980	(February 26) Israel and Egypt initiate formal diplomatic relations by exchanging ambassadors
1980	(July 30) Jerusalem proclaimed by Knesset the Eternal Capital of Israel
1981	(October 6) Sadat assassinated in Cairo

General Bibliography in English

The basic sources of the ancient history and topography of Jerusalem are the Bible and Josephus. Jerusalem figures prominently in the historical books of the Bible beginning with Samuel. The city is also referred to frequently in the Book of Psalms and in the prophetic books.

In *The Jewish War* by Flavius Josephus one finds detailed and reliable information by an eyewitness who lived through the war with Rome and carefully recorded what transpired.

The literature on Jerusalem is extensive. Only a small selection is listed in this bibliography. Some of the works that have been selected combine scholarly research with religious insight; some are only impressions of pious pilgrims or enthusiastic travellers. These widely different works are hardly equivalent, yet each item has its own value. Some of the works are lavishly illustrated and are treasured as works of art.[1]

Adler, Cyrus. *Memorandum on the Western Wall Submitted to the Special Commission of the League of Nations on behalf of the Rabbinate, the Jewish Agency for Palestine, et al.* Jerusalem: Azriel Press, 1930.

---

1. The illustrated works are marked by an asterisk.

Andrews, Fannie Fern. *The Holy Land Under Mandate*, 2 vols. Boston: Houghton Mifflin Co., 1931.

*Ashbee, C.R. ed. *Jerusalem 1918–1920*. London: The Pro Jerusalem Society, 1921 and *Jerusalem 1920–1922*. London: The Pro Jerusalem Society, 1924. Being the records of the Pro-Jerusalem Council during the period of the British Military Administration and the first two years of the British civil administration.

Avi-Yonah, Michael. *Jerusalem: The Saga of the Holy City*. Jerusalem: Universitas-Publishers, 1954.

Bahat, Dan. *Carta's Historical Atlas of Jerusalem*. Jerusalem: Carta, 1973.

Barclay, J.T. *The City of the Great King*. Philadelphia: J. Challen, 1857.

*Bartlett, W.H. *Walks About the City and Environs of Jerusalem*. London: George Virtue, 1844.

*———. *Jerusalem Revisited*. London: A. Hall, 1855.

Ben Arieh, Yehoshua. *A City Reflected in its Times; Jerusalem in the 19th Century*. Jerusalem: Yad Izhak Ben-Zvi Publications, 1977.

———. *Jerusalem in the 19th Century; The New City*. Jerusalem: Yad Izhak Ben-Zvi Institute, 1986.

Ben-Eliezer, Shimon. *Destruction and Renewal: The Synagogues of the Jewish Quarter*, 2nd rev. ed. Jerusalem: R. Mass, 1975.

Besant, Sir Walter and Palmer, E.H. *Jerusalem: The City of Herod and Saladin*. London: Chatto and Windus, 1889.

Bliss, Frederick Jones. *Excavations at Jerusalem, 1894–1897*. London: Committee of the Palestine Exploration Fund, 1898.

Blyth, Estelle. *When We Lived in Jerusalem*. London: Murray, 1927.

*Boudet, J. *Jerusalem: A History*. Ed. and trans. J. Boudet. New York: G.P. Putnam's Sons, 1967.

Campbell, G.A. *The Knights Templars*. London: Duckworth, 1937.

Casola, Pietro. *Canon Pietro Casola's Pilgrimage to Jerusalem in the Year 1494.* Trans. M. Margaret Newett. Manchester: University Press, 1907.

Clarke, Edward D. *Travels in Various Countries of Europe, Asia, and Africa,* 2 vols. London: Printed for T. Cadell and W. Davies, 1812.

Colbi, Saul P. *Christianity in the Holy Land: Past and Present.* Tel Aviv: Am Hasefer Publishing House, 1969.

Comay, Joan. *The Temple of Jerusalem.* London: Weidenfeld and Nicolson, 1975.

*Conder, Claude R. *Tent Work in Palestine,* 2 vols. London: The Committee of the Palestine Exploration Fund, 1878.

Fabri, Felix. "The Book of Wanderings of Brother Felix Fabri." Trans. from the Latin by Aubrey Stewart, in *Palestine Pilgrims' Text Society,* Vols. 7–10. London: Committee of the Palestine Exploration Fund, 1896.

Farmer, Leslie. *We Saw the Holy City.* London: Epworth Press, 1945.

*Fergusson, James. *An Essay on the Ancient Topography of Jerusalem.* London: Weale, 1847.

Finn, Elizabeth Anne. *Home in the Holy Land.* London: J. Nisbet, 1866.

Finn, James. *Stirring Times,* 2 vols. London: C. Kegan Paul, 1878.

Fosdick, Harry Emerson. *A Pilgrimage to Palestine.* New York: Macmillan, 1949.

Goitein, S.D. "The Sanctity of Jerusalem and Palestine in Early Islam." In *Studies in Islamic History and Institutions,* pp. 135–148. Leiden: E.J. Brill, 1966.

Goodrich-Freer, A. *Inner Jerusalem.* London: A. Constable, 1904.

Graham, Stephen. *With the Russian Pilgrims to Jerusalem.* London: Macmillan, 1913.

Gray, John. *A History of Jerusalem.* London: R. Hale, 1969.

Hanauer, J.E. *Walks In and Around Jerusalem.* London:

London Society for Promoting Christianity Amongst the Jews, 1926.

*Harper, Henry A. *Walks in Palestine*. London: The Religious Tract Society, 1888.

Harry, Myriam. *A Springtide in Palestine*. London: E. Benn, 1924.

Hirst, David and Beeson, Irene. *Sadat*. London: Faber and Faber Ltd., 1981.

Holmes, John Haynes. *Palestine Today and Tomorrow*. New York: Macmillan, 1929.

Holtz, Avraham. *The Holy City*. New York: W. W. Norton, 1971.

*Kendall, Henry. *Jerusalem City Plan: Preservation and Development During the British Mandate, 1918–1948*. London: H.M. Stationary Office, 1948.

Kenyon, Kathleen, M. *Jerusalem: Excavating 3,000 Years of History*. London: Thames and Hudson, 1967.

*Kinsel, Paschal and Henry, Leonard. *The Catholic Shrines of the Holy Land*. New York: Farrar, Straus and Young, 1952.

*Kollek, Teddy and Pearlman, Moshe. *Jerusalem: Sacred City of Mankind—A History of Forty Centuries*. Jerusalem: Steimatzky's Agency, 1968.

Lamartine, Alphonse Marie Louis de. *Recollections of the East*. Trans. Thomas Phipson, pp. 302–374. London: G. Virtue, 1845.

Lewis, T. Hayter. *The Holy Places of Jerusalem*. London: J. Murray, 1888.

Luke, Harry and Keith-Roach, Edward. *The Handbook of Palestine and Trans-Jordan*. London: Macmillan, 1934.

McDonald, James G. *My Mission in Israel 1948–1951*. London: V. Gollanez, 1951.

Macleod, Norman. *Eastward*. London: A. Strahan, 1866.

Malta Protestant College. *Journal of a Deputation* (Sent to the East by the Committee of the Malta Protestant College in 1849), 2 vols. London: J. Nisbet, 1854.

Maundrell, Henry. *A Journey From Aleppo to Jerusalem at Easter A.D. 1697*. London: White, 1810.

*Mazar, Benjamin. *The Mountain of the Lord: Excavating in Jerusalem*. New York: Doubleday, 1975.

Niccolo of Poggibonsi. *A Voyage Beyond the Seas*. Trans. Fr. T. Bellorini and Fr. E. Hoade. Jerusalem: Franciscan Press, 1945.

Oesterreicher, John M. and Sinai, Anne. *Jerusalem*. John M. Oesterreicher and Ann Sinai, eds. New York: J. Day Co., 1974.

*Olin, Stephen. *Travels in Egypt, Arabia Petraea, and the Holy Land*, 2 vols. New York: Harper and Bros., 1844.

Paassen, Pierre van. *Jerusalem Calling*. New York: Dial Press, 1950.

*Pococke, Richard. *A Description of the East and Some Other Countries*, 2 vols. London: Printed for the Author, 1743, 1745.

Porter, Josias Leslie. *The Giant Cities of Bashan and Syria's Holy Places*. New York: T. Nelson, 1871.

*———. *Jerusalem, Bethany, and Bethlehem*. London: T. Nelson, 1887.

Prawer, Joshua. *The Latin Kingdom of Jerusalem*. London: Weidenfeld and Nicolson, 1972.

———. *The World of the Crusaders*. London: Weidenfeld and Nicolson, 1972.

Rhodes, Albert. *Jerusalem As It Is*. London: J. Maxwell, 1865.

Robinson, Edward and Smith, E. *Biblical Researches in Palestine, Mt. Sinai, and Arabia Petraea*, 3 vols. Boston: Crocker and Brewster, 1841.

*Runciman, Steven. *A History of the Crusades*, 3 vols. New York: Harper and Row, 1964–1967.

*Sharon, Arieh. *Planning Jerusalem: The Old City and Its Environs*. New York: McGraw-Hill Book Co., 1973.

Smith, George Adam. *Jerusalem*, 2 vols. New York: Ktav Publishing House, 1972.

*Steckoll, Solomon. *The Temple Mount*. London: T. Stacey, 1972.

Storrs, Ronald. *Orientations*. London: Nicholson and Watson, 1937.

Thackeray, William Makepeace. *Notes of a Journey From Cornhill to Grand Cairo*. London: Chapman and Hall, 1846.

Thompson, Charles. *The Travels of the Late Charles Thompson*, 3 vols. London: J. Robinson, 1744.

Thomson, Andrew. *In the Holy Land*. London: T. Nelson, 1886.

Thomson, W.M. *The Land and the Book*. London: T. Nelson, 1911.

Twain, Mark. *The Innocents Abroad*. New York: Harper and Bros., 1911.

Van Dyke, Henry. *Out-of-Doors in the Holy Land*. London: Holder, 1908.

Vester, Bertha Stafford. *Our Jerusalem: An American Family in the Holy City 1881–1949*. London: Evans Brothers Ltd., 1951.

Wallace, Edwin Sherman. *Jerusalem the Holy*. Edinburgh: Oliphant, Andersin and Ferrier, 1898.

———. *The Temple or the Tomb*. London: R. Bentley, 1880.

Warren, Charles. *Underground Jerusalem*. London: R. Bentley, 1876.

Williams, George. *The Holy City*, 2 vols. London: Parker, 1849.

Wilson, Charles W. *Golgotha and the Holy Sepulchre*. London: Committee of the Palestine Exploration Fund, 1906.

———. *Jerusalem the Holy City*. London: J.S. Virtue, 1888.

———. *The Recovery of Jerusalem*. London: R. Bentley, 1871.

Reference
Bibliography

Hoade, Eugene. *Western Pilgrims*. Jerusalem: Franciscan Press, 1952—A "list of the principal works in English on the Holy Land up to the beginning of the present century."

Robinson, Edward and Smith E. *Biblical Researches in Palestine, Mount Sinai, and Arabia Petraea*. Boston: Crocker and Brewster, 1841. First Appendix, pp. 4–28—A "Chronological list of works on Palestine and Mount Sinai."

Rohricht, Reinhold, and Meisner, Heinrich. *Bibliotheca Geographica Palaestinae*. Enlarged and brought up to date by David H.K. Amiram. Jerusalem: Universitas Booksellers, 1963.

———. *Deutsche Pilgerreisen nach dem Heiligen Lande*. Berlin: Weidmannsche Buchhandlung, 1880—One thousand items, spanning the years 333 to 1878, are listed and annotated in German.

Thomsen, Peter. *Die Palastina—Literatur*, 7 vols. Leipzig: J.C. Hinrichs, 1911–1972—An international bibliographical listing of works related to Palestine from the year 1878 to 1945.

Tobler, Titus. *Bibliographia Geographica Palaestinae*. Leipzig: S. Hirzel, 1867—A listing of works dealing with travel in the Holy Land, with critical annotations, arranged by year of travel.

Index

Abd-al-Malik (Caliph), xxiii, 58, 59
Abdullah (k. of Transjordan), 151, 158, 161, 162
Abrahams, Israel, 31–32, 43
Agrippa (k.), 29–30
Akiba, 39
Al-Aqsa Mosque
appropriation of, 71
construction of, xxiii, xxiv, 59–60
conversion of, to Christianity, 66
fire in, 180
Alexander the Great, Jerusalem and, 17–18
Allenby, Edmund Henry, 139, 140, 151
Antiochus IV, 19
Anti-Semitism, Zionism and, 130
Anti-Zionism, 134, 142
Arab-Israeli wars
1948–1949, 157–158, 162

Six-Day War (1967), 167, 168, 171, 173–174, 177, 185
Yom Kippur War (1973), 199
Arabs. See Islam
Architecture
Crusaders, 73–74
Mamelukes and, 87–88
Ottoman Turks and, 95–96
Arius, 48
Ark of the Covenant
loss of, 16–17
moved to Jerusalem, 5–6, 7
Armistice Agreement, 163, 171
Artisans, 125–126
Ashbee, C. R., 147, 178, 187
al-Ashraf Khalil (Sultan of Egypt), 86
Assyrians, Israel conquered by, 9–10

Babylonian Empire
    fall of, 16
    Jerusalem conquered by,
        12–13
Babylonian exile, Jerusalem
    and, 15–16
Baibars (Sultan of Egypt),
    86
Baldwin II (k. of Jerusalem),
    70, 75
Baldwin (k. of Jerusalem),
    69–70
Balfour, Arthur James, 139,
    150
Balfour Declaration, 139,
    141, 142, 153, 155
Balkans, Ottoman Turks
    and, 119
Bar Kokhba revolt, Roman
    Empire and, 38–40, 44
Basle Program, 132
Begin, Menahem, 201
Beha ed-din, 79
Ben-Gurion, David, 133,
    162
Bevin, Ernest, 156
Birobidzhan, xviii–xix
Brennan, Joseph P., 179
Britain. See United
    Kingdom
Byzantine Empire, Ottoman
    Turks and, 94

Caligula (e. of Rome), 29
Canaanites, 12
Chosroes (k. of Persia), 53

Christianity
    Egypt and, 106
    Islam and, 58–59, 61
    Jerusalem and, xi, xviii,
        xix–xxi, 47–53
    Judaism and, 121–122
    Latin Kingdom
        fall of, 77–84
        rise of, 63–76
    Ottoman Turks and, 94,
        98–99
Church of the Holy
    Sepulchre, fire in,
    102–103, 165–166
Clemens VI (pope of Rome),
    89
Colbi, Saul, 212
Congress of Berlin (1878),
    118, 119
Constantine (Grand Duke
    of Russia), 113
Constantine I (e. of Rome),
    44, 47–51
Constantine IX (e. of Rome),
    62
Constantinople, fall of, 94
Corruption
    Crusaders, 74–76, 82
    Janissaries, 94
    Ottoman Turks and, 96–
        97, 101
Council of Chalcedon (451
    C.E.), 68
Council of Nicaea (325), 48
Crimean War, 107–108,
    117–118

Crusades
  first, 63–76
  fourth, 81
  Frederick II (e. of Ger-
    many), 82–83
  Jerusalem and, xx–xxi, 62
  Mamelukes and, 86–87
  second, 77–81
  third, 81
Cunningham, Alan Gordon,
  149
Cyprus, United Kingdom
  and, 137
Cyrus (k. of Persia), 16

Daimbert (Patriarch of
  Jerusalem), 69
David (King), Jerusalem
  and, 2, 4–6
Djemal Pasha, 138
Dome of the Rock
  construction of, xxiii,
    xxiv, 58–59
  conversion of, to Chris-
    tianity, 66
Dreyfus, Alfred, 131
Dreyfus Case, 130, 131

Eban, Abba, 173, 175
Edict of Toleration (1856),
  111, 118
Egypt
  Israel (modern state) and,
    200–204
  Jerusalem and, 106

Khorasmian Turks and,
  83
Mameluke rule, 85–86
Six-Day War (1967), 173
Soviet Union and,
  199–200
Yom Kippur War (1973),
  199
Eshkol, Levi, 173
Europe. See also entries
  under names of
  countries
  Jerusalem, nineteenth
    century, 105–106,
    109–119
  Ottoman Turks and,
    106–107
  World War I, Middle East
    and, 138–140
Ezra (leader), 17

Fabri, Felix, 88
Farmer, Leslie, 104
Feudalism, Latin Jerusalem,
  67
Finley, John, 139
Finn, James, 110, 138
First Crusade, 63–76
Flavius Claudius Julianus
  (e. of Rome), 50. See
  Julian the Apostate
Fosdick, Harry Emerson, 22
Fourth Crusade, 81
France
  Crimean War, 117–118
  Dreyfus Case, 130, 131

France (*continued*)
  Franco-Prussian War, 114
  Jerusalem and, 107,
    111–112
  Ottoman Turks and, 108
Franciscan Order, 89–90
Francis I (k. of France), 111
Francis Joseph (e. of
    Austria-Hungary), 125
Francis of Assisi, Saint, 89
Franco-Prussian War, 114
Frederick II (e. of Germany),
    82–83

Gaon of Vilna, 100
Geddes, Patrick, 146
Georgians, 89
Germany
  Jerusalem and, 107,
    114–115
  Ottoman Turks and,
    137–138
Godfrey of Bouillon, 65, 67,
    69
God-human relationship
  Jerusalem and, xv
  Temple and, 12–13
Great Schism (1054 C.E.),
    68
Greece
  Jerusalem and, 18–19
  revolt of, 119
Greek Orthodox church,
    Ottoman Turks and,
    98–99

Hadrian (e. of Rome), 43,
    44, 52
al-Hakim (Caliph of
    Baghdad), 61–62
al-Harizi, 81, 90
Hasmonean kingdom
  fall of, 21, 22
  Jerusalem, 19–20
Hellenistic empire. *See*
    Greece
Heraclius (e. of Rome), 53,
    55
Herod (King)
  death of, 29
  Jerusalem and, 22–27
Herzl, Theodor, 131–133,
    170
Hezekiah (King), 11
Hitler, Adolph, 153
Holocaust, 32, 169–170
Hospitallers, 70–71, 72, 76,
    78
Humbert, Cardinal, 68
al-Husseini, Hajj Amin
    (Grand Mufti of
    Jerusalem), 152–153,
    155
Hussein (k. of Jordan), 151,
    161, 162, 174

Ibrahim Pasha, 106, 117,
    188
Internationalization, of
    Jerusalem, xxi, 157–
    158, 160, 205–208

Isaiah (prophet), Jerusalem
   and, 11
Islam
   British Mandate, 153
   Janissaries and, 93–94
   Jerusalem and, xi–xii, xvi,
      xxi–xxiv, 55–62,
      81–82
   Ottoman Turks and,
      100–101
   United Kingdom and, 141
   Zionism and, 142
Israel (ancient), Assyrians
   conquer, 9–10
Israel (modern state)
   Egypt and, 200–204
   Jerusalem administration,
      210–215
   proclamation of, 156
   Six-Day War (1967), 173
   United Nations and, 157

James the Less, 48
Janissaries, Ottoman Turks,
   93–94
Jarvis, James, 151
Jeremiah (prophet), Jeru-
   salem and, 11
Jerusalem
   Alexander the Great and,
      17–18
   in antiquity, 1–8
   Babylonian exile, 15–16
   Christianity and, xix–xxi,
      47–53

   chronology of, 223–226
   current conditions in,
      195–198
   divided rule of, 157–171
   Frederick II (e. of Ger-
      many) and, 82–83
   future of, 208–209
   Greece and, 18–19
   Hasmonean kingdom,
      19–20
   Herod and, 22–27
   hope and concerns for,
      199–205
   internationalization,
      205–208
   Islam and, xxi–xxiv, 55–
      62, 81–82
   Israeli administration of,
      210–215
   Judaism and, xi, xii–xix
   Latin Kingdom
      fall of, 77–84
      rise of, 63–76
   Mameluke rule, 85–91
   nineteenth century
      European powers,
      105–119
      Jewish growth in,
      121–126
   origin of name, 2
   Ottoman Turkish rule of,
      93–104
   partition and fall of, 9–13
   Persian hegemony, 17
   reunification of, 173–191

Jerusalem (*continued*)
  Roman conquest of,
    32–35
  Roman rule of, 29–30,
    37–38, 41–45
  Seljuk Turks conquer, 62
  survival and rebirth of,
    xxiv–xxv
  United Kingdom mandate
    in, 137–156
  world religions and, xi–xii
  Zionism and, 127–135
Jesus, Jerusalem and, 23, 48
Joab, 5
Jordan, 158, 160, 163–167,
    171, 178, 185
Josephus, 18, 31, 187
Joshua, 5
  Jerusalem and, 2
Judah He-Hasid, 100
Judah he-Hasid, 165
Judah (Kingdom)
  described, 9
  fall of, 11–12
  survival of, 10
Judaism
  Christianity and, 121–122
  Egypt and, 106
  Jerusalem and, xi, xii–xix,
    121–126
  Mameluke rule and, 90
  martyrdom, Crusades
    and, 63–64
  Ottoman Turks and, 98,
    99–100

Roman conquest and,
    33–34
Saladin and, 80–81
Julian the Apostate (e. of
    Rome), 50–51
Julius Severus (Roman
    general), 39

Khorasmian Turks, 83
Knights Templars, 68, 70,
    71–72, 76, 78, 115
Kollek, Teddy, 189, 197

Lamartine, Alphonse de,
    103–104
Latin Kingdom
  fall of, 77–84
  Mamelukes and, 86–87
  rise of, 63–76
Latin Patriarchate, revival
    of, 112
Lawrence, T. E., 140
Lillian, Ephraim, 125
London Society for Pro-
    moting Christianity
    Among the Jews, 110

Macleod, Norman, 206–207
Maimonides, Moses, xiv
Mameluke rule, of Jeru-
    salem, xxiv, 85–91, 95
al-Mamun, Abdullah, 59
Mandate for Palestine,
    142–156
Mark Anthony, 23

Martyrdom, Crusades and, 63–64, 66
Massadah, 65
Mecca, Islam and, xvi, 58, 60
Medina, Islam and, 58, 60
Meir, Golda, 211
Messianism
    Bar Kokhba revolt, 38–40
    Jerusalem and, xiv–xv
Mohammed II (the Conqueror, Sultan of Turkey), 94–95
Monarchy, establishment of, 4
Mongol invasion (1260), 86, 91
Montefiore, Moses, 122–124
Moslems. *See* Islam
Mount of Olives cemetery, xii, 91
Mubarak, Hosni, 204
Murad IV (Sultan of Turkey), 101

Nachmanides, 90–91
Napoleon (e. of France), 96, 103, 105
Napoleonic wars, 103
Nasser, Abdul Gamal, 173, 199
Nehemiah (leader), 17

Oesterreicher, John M., 164
Omar (Caliph), xxiii, xxiv, 56, 57, 60, 79

Ottoman Turks
    Balkans and, 119
    Crimean War, 117–118
    European powers and, 106–107, 111
    France and, 108
    Jerusalem ruled by, 93–104
    Russia and, 117, 118
    United Kingdom and, 137
    World War I, 139
    Zionism and, 135
Ovadia of Bertinoro, 91

Paganism, 41–45
Palestine
    Mandate for Palestine, 142–156
    Zionism and, 132
Paul VI (pope of Rome), 171
Persia
    Babylonian Empire and, 16
    Jerusalem and, 17, 53
    Ottoman Turks and, 95
Philistines, 4
Pilgrimage, to Jerusalem, xvi, xx, xxiii, 60, 98, 99, 112, 167–168, 171
Pius IX (pope of Rome), 112
Postal system, 109
Prophets
    Jerusalem and, 11, 12
    Judah (Kingdom) and, 10
Prussia, Jerusalem and, 117

Railroad construction, 125
Ramban. *See* Nachmanides
Redclife, Stratford de, 111
Reform Judaism, anti-
    Zionism, 134
Rehoboam (King), 9
Rhineland, Jewish massacres
    in, 64
Richard I (k. of England),
    81
Road building, 124–125,
    144–145
Robinson, Edward, 184,
    187
Rohan, Michael, 180
Roman Empire
    Bar Kokhba revolt, 38–40
    Hasmonean kingdom
        and, 21
    Jerusalem conquered by,
        xiv, 32–35
    Jerusalem ruled by, 29–
        30, 41–45
    revolt against, 30–31
Rothschild, Walter, 139
Russia, xviii. *See also*
    Soviet Union
    Crimean War, 117–118
    Jerusalem and, 107, 109–
        110, 112–114
    Ottoman Turks and, 101,
        102, 117, 118
    Zionism, 130–131
Russo-Turkish War (1877–
    1878), 118

al-Sadat, Anwar, 199–204
Saladin (Sultan), 77–78, 79,
    80–81, 84, 90, 180
Samaritans, 3
Samuel, Herbert, 143–144
Samuel (prophet), leader-
    ship of, 4
Sardinia, Jerusalem and, 117
Saul (King), politics and, 4
Schatz, Boris, 125
Second Crusade, 77–81
Second Temple. *See* Temple
    (Second)
Selim I (Sultan of Turkey),
    95
Seljuk Turks, Jerusalem
    conquered by, 62, 64
Shafiq Islambouli, Khalid,
    204
Sharon, Arieh, 214
Six-Day War (1967), xxiv,
    167, 168, 171, 173–
    174, 177, 185
Smith, George Adam, 74,
    198
Solomon (King)
    achievements of, 8
    Herod compared, 26
    Temple constructed by,
        6–7
Soviet Union, Egypt and,
    199–200. *See also*
    Russia
Spain
    Jerusalem and, 117
    Jews expelled from, 91

Stafford, Horatio, 116
Stations of the Cross,
    Jerusalem and, 23
Storrs, Ronald, 140, 141,
    145, 146, 147, 187, 195
Suez Canal, 125, 137
Suleiman the Magnificent
    (Sultan of Turkey),
    xxiv, 95–96, 101, 108,
    109, 111
Symeon (Patriarch of
    Jerusalem), 68
Synagogue
    institution of, 16
    Temple and, 34
Syria, Yom Kippur War
    (1973), 199

Templars. See Knights
    Templars
Temple Mount
    Christianity and, 52–53
    Islam and, xxii, xxiii,
        57–59
    Judaism and, xv, xvi, xviii
Temple (Second)
    construction of, 16
    internalization of, 33–34
    reconstruction of, 23–27
    Rome destroys, 32, 33
Temple (Solomon's)
    Babylonians destroy,
        12–13
    constructed by Solomon
        (King), 6–7

Ten Commandments
    loss of, 16–17
    move to Jerusalem, 5–6, 7
Thackeray, William
    Makepeace, 125
Theodosius the Great (e. of
    Rome), 50, 51–52
Third Crusade, 81
Titus, 31, 32, 37
Touro, Judah, 123
Treaties of the Capitulation,
    108–109, 111
Treaty of Paris (1856),
    107–108
Truman, Harry S., 163
Turks. See Ottoman Turks

Uganda Plan, xviii–xix, 132
United Kingdom, xviii
    Crimean War, 117–118
    Jerusalem and, 115, 137–
        156, 166
    Judaism and, 110–111
United Nations
    Israel and, 157
    Jerusalem and, xxi, 160,
        162, 175–176
    Mandate for Palestine,
        142
United States
    anti-Zionism, 134
    Israel and, 162–163
    Jerusalem and, 115–117
Urban II (pope of Rome),
    63, 64, 65, 67
Uru-Salem, 2

Vatican, Jerusalem and, xxi
Vespasian (e. of Rome),
    30–31
Vienna, siege of, 102

al-Walid (Caliph), 58
Warren, Charles, 24
Weizmann, Chaim, 188
White Paper (1939),
    155–156
Wilhelm II (k. of Germany),
    114–115, 140
William of Tyre, 66
Williams, George, 79–80,
    102–103

Wingate, Charles Orde, 143
World War I, 138–140, 141
World War II, 115, 153

Yemenite Jews, Jerusalem
    and, 115–116
Yohanan ben Zakkai, 100
Yom Kippur War (1973),
    199

Zionism
    rise of, 127–135
    World War I, Middle East
        and, 138–140, 141
Zunz, Leopold, 128

About the Author

Rabbi Abraham E. Millgram was ordained at the Jewish Theological Seminary of America and received his doctorate in History from Dropsie University. After serving in pulpits in Wilmington and Philadelphia, he founded the Hillel Foundation at the University of Minnesota, serving as its first director. He was Educational Director of the United Synagogue for Conservative Judaism, where he developed curricula, published textbooks, and guided all schools affiliated with the Conservative Movement. He authored numerous books, including *Jewish Worship* (which received the Best Book of the Year Award of the Jewish Book Council), *Sabbath: Day of Delight*, and *Jerusalem Curiosities*. He was a resident of Jerusalem for thirty-seven years before passing away at the age of 98.